NATO MAJOR WARSHIPS — EUROPE

A Tri-Service Pocketbook

The Tri-Service Pocketbook Series

The Air Series

NATO Major Combat Aircraft
Soviet and East European Major Combat Aircraft
Commercial Transport Aircraft

The Naval Series

NATO Major Warships — Europe
NATO Major Warships — USA and Canada
Soviet and East European Major Warships
Major Warships — Asia, Africa, Australasia and Latin America
The World's Small Warships

The Military Series

Main Battle Tanks
Light Tanks, Armoured Cars and Reconnaissance Vehicles
APCs and MCVs
Artillery Systems
Soft-Skinned Vehicles
Anti-Tank Systems
Air Defence Systems
Pistols and Sub-Machine Guns
Machine Guns and Rifles
Battlefield Electronic Systems
Battlefield Mobility Equipment
Battlefield Close Air Support
Infantry Support Systems
Bomb Disposal, Detection and Anti-Riot Equipment
Surveillance and Perimeter Protection Equipment
Internal Security Vehicles
Communications Equipment

NATO MAJOR WARSHIPS — EUROPE

Eric J. Grove

A Tri-Service Pocketbook

TRI-SERVICE

PRESS

First published by Tri-Service Press Limited, 42/43 Lower Marsh, London SE1 7RQ

British Library Cataloguing in Publication Data

Grove, Eric
NATO major warships — Europe
1 North Atlantic Treaty Organization navies. Warships
I. Title
623.8′25′091821

ISBN 1-85400-006-3

Distribution in the United States by Howell Press, Inc.,
700 Harris Street, Suite B, Charlottesville, Virginia 22901.
Telephone (804) 977-4006.

Typeset by Florencetype Ltd, Kewstoke, Avon
Printed and bound in the United Kingdom

Notes on tables

Dimensions: length is always given overall.
Torpedoes: HWT heavyweight torpedo, LWT lightweight torpedo.
Sonar: low frequency is below 3kHz, medium frequency 3–10 kHz, high frequency above 10 kHz.
Radar Bands: E 2–3 gHz, F 3–4 gHz, G 4–6 gHz, H 6–9 gHz, I 9–10, J 10–20 gHz.

Introduction

This pocketbook covers the major warships of the European signatories of the North Atlantic Alliance. Although French and Spanish units are not as automatically subject to the control of NATO commanders as the other members' warships, all the NATO navies work closely together when required, and both French and Spanish ships have played a full part in recent NATO exercises. Both France and Spain along with Britain, the Netherlands, Belgium, West Germany, Italy and Portugal are also full members of the Western European Union. The contribution of Western Europe's naval forces to European security is easily underestimated. As the following pages show there is a massive panoply of naval power at Europe's disposal with all types of warship represented. Navies have little to fear from the new era of improved East-West relations. Arms control on land and in the air on the Continent should mean even more stress on maritime re-inforcement, a greater importance for limited uses of force out of area and more resources relatively for naval purposes.

The order of the types of unit in this book is deliberate and reflects the author's ideas on the relative importance of each category. SSBNs stand alone in their specialised role, followed by SSNs and carriers as joint 'capital ships' of naval warfare proper. Then come the surface combatants in various shapes and sizes, with the main criterion being to include all vessels with cruiser (C), destroyer (D) or frigate (F) pennant numbers. Then come conventional submarines increasingly useful only against surface units and then the major amphibious ships which while not directly combatant in themselves provide a vital maritime power projection capability that will be increasingly in demand.

Eric J. Grove is a well-known naval authority and historian, highly regarded for his analytical expertise. In this series he brings together all his experience and contacts to provide the very latest information on the world's in-service navies. His other books are: *Vanguard to Trident: British Naval Policy Since World War II*; *The Future of Sea Power*; *Sea Battles in Close-up*; *NATO's Defence of the North*.
He has held appointments as Curlian Lecturer, RN College Dartmouth, 1971 (Deputy Director of Strategic Studies 1982–4). Exchange Professor USN Annapolis, 1980–81, worked with the Council for Arms Control 1985–6; since 1986 freelance defence writer and consultant; helped establish the Foundation for International Security of which he is now the Naval Research Director.

Author's acknowledgements Thanks must be given to Dr and Mrs G.E.B. Grove, who gave essential assistance with compilation and word processing, and to Linda Cullen and Mary Beth Straight of the US Naval Institute, David Foxwell of *Naval Forces* and A.J. Watts of *Navy International* for enormous help in finding photographs.

Abbreviations

A	auxiliary
AA	anti-aircraft
ADAWS	action data automation weapons system
AEW	airborne early warning
ASW	anti-submarine warfare
ASROC	anti-submarine rocket
C	cruiser
CAAIS	computer-assisted action information system
CACS	computer-assisted command system
CINCHAN	Commander in Chief Channel
CIWS	close-in weapon system
CNR	Cantieri Navali Riuniti
CNT	Cantieri Navali del Tirreno
CODOG	combined diesel or gas turbine
CODLAG	combined diesel electric and gas turbine
CRDA	Cantireri Riuniti dell'Adriatico
CVS	anti-submarine support aircraft carrier
CVSA	anti-submarine/attack aircraft carrier
D	destroyer
DASH	drone anti-submarine helicopter
DM	destroyer minelayer
ECM	electronic countermeasures
ER	extended range
ESM	electronic support measure (i.e. emissions receiver)
F	frigate
FFG	guided missile frigate
FRAM	Fleet Rehabilitation And Modernisation programme
HDW	Howaldtswerke Deutsche Werft
hp	horsepower
HWT	heavyweight torpedo
L	landing vessel
LCM	landing craft mechanised
LCT	landing craft tank
LCVP	landing craft vehicle and personnel
LCU	landing craft utility
LPD	landing platform dock
LSD	landing ship dock
LWT	lightweight torpedo
MIRV	multiple independently targetable re-entry vehicle
mm	millimetres
MR	medium range
NATO	North Atlantic Treaty Organisation
NAUTIS	naval autonomous information system
NFR	NATO frigate replacement
NTDS	naval tactical data system
PBV	post boost vehicle

R	aircraft carrier
RFA	Royal Fleet Auxiliary
RN	Royal Navy
S	submarine
SAM	surface-to-air missile
SATIR	System zur Auswertung Taktischer Informationen auf Raketenzerstören
SENIT	Système d'Exploitation Navale des Informations Tactiques
shp	shaft horsepower
SLBM	submarine launched ballistic missile
SSBN	nuclear powered ballistic missile submarine
SSC	coastal conventionally powered submarine
SSK	conventionally powered hunter-killer submarine
SSM	surface-to-surface missile
SSN	nuclear powered attack submarine
STOVL	short take-off vertical landing
STWS	shipborne torpedo weapon system
USS	United States Ship
VDS	Variable Depth Sonar
VLF	very low frequency
VBEL	Vickers Shipbuilding and Engineering Ltd.
VTOL	vertical take-off and landing

Number in class: 1

L'INFLEXIBLE S615 1985

Specifications and Technical Data

Ballistic Missile Submarine (SSBN)

L'Inflexible Class

Displacement, tonnes: 8,920 submerged
Dimensions, metres (feet): 128.7 × 10.6 × 10 (422.1 × 34.8 × 32.8)
Missiles: 16 × M-4 ballistic missiles
Torpedo tubes: 4 × 533 mm forward
Sonar: DSUV 61 towed array, DSUX 21 multifunction hull array, DUUX 5 passive ranging and intercept hull array
Radar: DRUA 33 I band search
Machinery: 1 × pressurised water reactor, 2 × geared steam turbines, 1 × shaft, 16,000 hp; diesel electric-battery auxiliary propulsion
Speed, knots: 25
Range, nautical miles: limited only by endurance of crew; 5,000 at 4 knots on auxiliary propulsion
Complement: 127

Photograph: *L'Inflexible* (Jean Biaugeaud/USNI)

France's sixth SSBN (in French SNLE — Sous-Marin Nucléaire Lance Engins), the boat was announced in September 1978 and laid down in the Naval Dockyard, Cherbourg in March 1980. Launched in June 1982, she began her first patrol in May 1985. A sixth SSBN was required in order to allow three submarines to be maintained on patrol. *L'Inflexible* was the first submarine to carry the M-4 submarine launched ballistic missile. This carries the TN-70 Multiple Independently Targetable Re-entry Vehicle (MIRV) front end with six 150 kiloton warheads. The M-4's warhead 'footprint', ie the area in which targets for an individual missile must be found, is reportedly 150 × 350 kilometres over its maximum range of 4,000 kilometres. M-4's dimensions are 11.5 × 1.93 metres. *L'Inflexible* is an evolutionary development of the previous 'Le Redoutable' class. The boat has a quieter propulsion system and can dive down to 300 metres. The main recognition feature is a more streamlined sail structure with higher-mounted diving planes. For self-defence against both surface and sub-surface threats the submarine carries at least twelve L-5 homing torpedoes and SM-39 Exocet anti-ship missiles. The M-4 system will be replaced by the modified M-45 missile with a longer range of 5,000 kilometres and improved TN-71 warheads. *L'Inflexible* is due to remain in service until the year 2012 and she will be fitted with the M-5 missile, due into service at the end of the century. As with all Western SSBNs two crews are assigned to the boat.

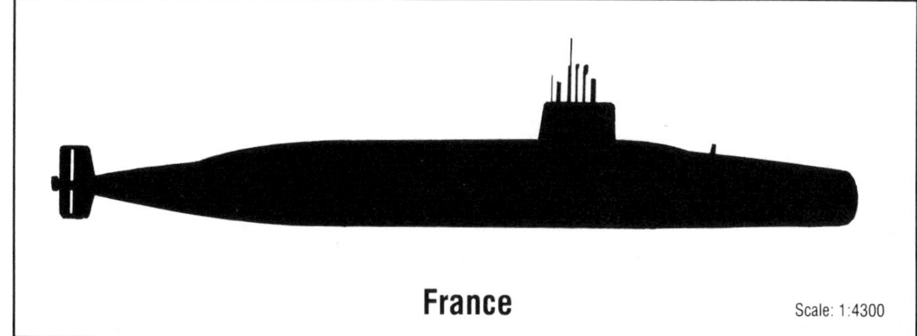

Le Redoutable Class

Specifications and Technical Data

Number in class: 5

LE REDOUTABLE S611 1971
LE TERRIBLE S612 1973
LE FOUDROYANT S610 1974
L'INDOMPTABLE S613 1976
LE TONNANT S614 1980

Displacement, tonnes: 8,940 submerged
Dimensions, metres (feet): 128 × 10.6 × 10 (419.9 × 34.8 × 32.8)
Missiles: 16 × M-4 or M-20 ballistic missiles
Torpedo tubes: 4 × 550 mm forward
Sonar: DUUV 23 low-frequency passive search panoramic array or (modernised boats) DSUX 21 multifunction hull array, DUUX 2 or 5 passive ranging and intercept hull array
Radar: DRUA 33 I band search
Machinery: 1 × pressurised water reactor, 2 × geared steam turbines, 1 × shaft, 16,000 hp; diesel electric-battery auxiliary propulsion
Speed, knots: 20
Range, nautical miles: limited only by endurance of crew; 5,000 at 4 knots on auxiliary propulsion
Complement: 135

Le Redoutable, laid down in November 1964, was the first SSBN authorised in 1963 in order to provide the French 'Force de Dissuasion' with a strategic 'triad' of nuclear bombers, land-based missiles and submarine-launched ballistic missiles. She and her four sisters were all built at the Naval Dockyard, Cherbourg. The class is currently being modernised with new M-4 missile and other equipment to a similar standard to the sixth French SSBN *L'Inflexible*, which the modernised boats resemble with their reshaped hulls. The first boat to be modernised was *Le Tonnant* from 1985 to 1988, followed by *L'Indomptable*, which completed her conversion in 1989. *Le Terrible* is due to be converted by 1991 and *Le Foudroyant* by 1993. *Le Redoutable* herself will not undergo conversion, instead she will be replaced in the mid-1990s by a totally new SSBN, *Le Triomphant*. Unconverted boats carry the M-20 missile with a range of 3,000 kilometres and a 1-2 megaton thermonuclear warhead: the M-20 is 10.4 × 1.5 metres. The M-20 is fired from the missile tube by compressed air unlike the bigger M-4 which is launched from the tube by a combustible charge. For self-defence the 'Le Redoutable' class carry a mix of up to eighteen 533 mm homing torpedoes, L-5 anti-submarine/anti-surface weapons and F-17s for anti-surface ship use: SM-39 Exocet missiles may replace the latter in due course. Maximum diving depth is reported as 250 metres. The French SSBN force is based at a specially constructed facility at L'Isle Longue to the south of Brest.

Photograph: Le Redoutable Class (ECP Armées/Naval Forces)

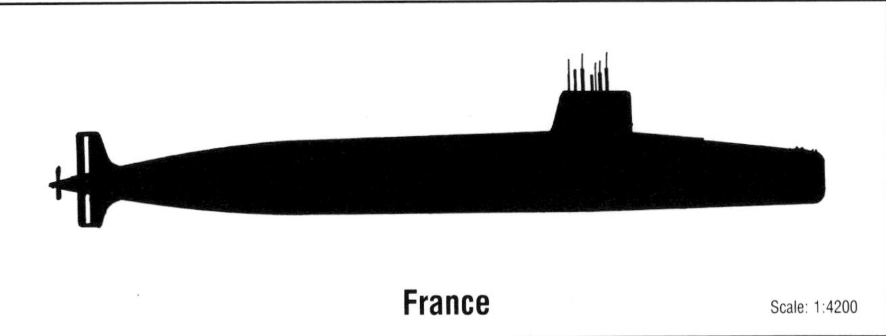

Specifications and Technical Data

Number in class: 4

RESOLUTION S22 1967
REPULSE S23 1968
RENOWN S26 1968
REVENGE S27 1969

Resolution Class

Displacement, tonnes: 8,500 submerged
Dimensions, metres (feet): 129.5 × 10.1 × 9.2 (425 × 33 × 30)
Missiles: 16 × Polaris A-3TK ballistic missiles
Torpedo tubes: 6 × 533 mm forward
Sonar: 2046 towed array, 2001 low-frequency active/passive bow array, 2007 hull-mounted high/medium-frequency passive flank array, 2019 passive/active ranging and intercept
Radar: 1006 I band navigation
Machinery: 1 × PWR 1 nuclear reactor, 2 × geared steam turbines, 1 × shaft, 15,000 hp, diesel electric-battery auxiliary propulsion
Speed, knots: 25
Range, nautical miles: limited only by endurance of crew
Complement: 143

Photograph: *Repulse* at completion (VSEL)

Ordered in 1963 following the previous year's Nassau Agreement on the provision of American Polaris missiles to the UK, *Resolution* and *Repulse* were built by Vickers at Barrow-in-Furness and *Renown* and *Revenge* by Cammell Laird at Birkenhead. *Resolution* and *Renown* were laid down in 1964 and *Repulse* and *Revenge* in 1965. The design was based on the 'Valiant' class SSN. A fifth boat was projected, but was cancelled in 1965. In 1969 the maintenance of Britain's nuclear deterrent was officially passed to the Polaris submarines and since June that year one British SSBN has been on patrol at all times. In order to penetrate Moscow's anti-ballistic missile defences, the 4,600 kilometre range Polaris missiles were fitted with new Chevaline front ends. *Renown* received the new missiles in 1982, *Resolution* in 1984, *Repulse* in 1986 and *Revenge* in 1988. Chevaline seems to consist of a post-boost vehicle normally carrying two 200 kiloton warheads and a number of balloon decoys. Both PBV and warheads are British. A single submarine reportedly targets all its missiles at the Soviet capital. The submarines are based at Faslane on Loch Long, Scotland. The 'Resolution' class is to be replaced in the 1990s by four new 15,000 ton 'Vanguard' class SSBNs, each of which will carry 16 Trident D-5 SLBMs maintained in the USA. *Vanguard* was ordered in 1986 and *Victorious* in 1987. The 'Resolutions' carry Mk 24 Tigerfish torpedoes for self defence.

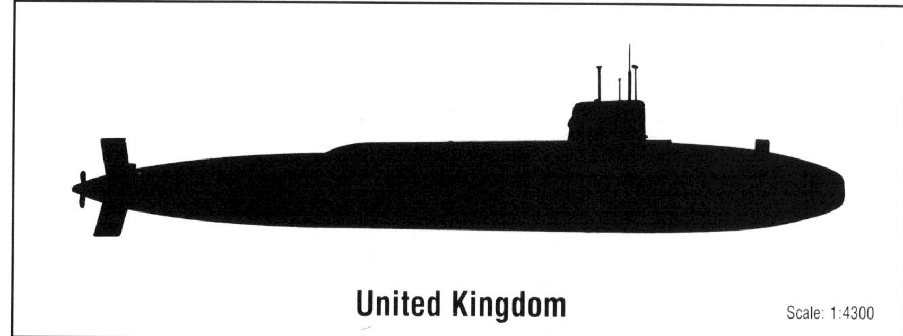

United Kingdom

Scale: 1:4300

Nuclear-Powered Attack Submarines (SSN)

Rubis Class

Number in class: 5

RUBIS S601 1983
SAPHIR S602 1984
CASABIANCA S603 1987
ÉMERAUDE S604 1988
AMÉTHYSTE S605 1991

Specifications and Technical Data

Displacement, tonnes: 2,670 submerged
Dimensions, metres (feet): 72.1 × 7.6 × 6.4 (236.5 × 24.9 × 21)
Torpedo tubes: 4 × 533 mm forward
Sonar: DSUV 62 towed array, DUUA 2B medium-frequency active hull array, DSUV 22 low-frequency passive search array, DUUX 5 passive ranging and warning
Radar: DRUA 33 I band search
Action Information Organisation: SADE
Machinery: 1 × 48 megawatt pressurised water reactor, 2 × turbo alternators, 1 × electric motor and shaft, 9,500 hp; diesel electric-battery auxiliary propulsion
Speed, knots: 25
Range, nautical miles: limited only by endurance of crew, normally 45 days
Complement: 65

France's SNAs (Sous-Marin Nucléaire d'Attaque) are the smallest operational SSNs in the world. Based at Toulon in the Mediterranean, they are optimised for anti-surface ship warfare and carry a mix of 14 L-5 and F-17 torpedoes and SM-39 Exocet anti-ship missiles. Alternatively, up to 32 mines may be carried. The boats are reportedly relatively slow and noisy and the four original units are to be modified along the lines of the fifth submarine *Améthyste*. This name is an acronym for 'AMélioration Tactique HYdrodynamique Silence Transmission Écoute', a programme to reduce radiated noise, especially from the power plant. This will make the boats much more effective anti-submarine units. *Améthyste* will have a new natural circulation reactor as well as a longer hull and more streamlined superstructure. A new multi-function hull sonar array will also be fitted and a new combat data system. Two more 'Améthyste' boats have been laid down, one in 1987, the other in 1988 and a fourth is projected. These boats will have an endurance of 90 days and a complement of 66. All France's SNAs are built at the Naval Dockyard, Cherbourg. *Rubis* was laid down (with the original name *Provence*) in 1976 and *Saphir* (as *Bretagne*) in 1979; the names were changed in 1980. *Casabianca* was laid down in 1981, *Émeraude* in 1982 and *Améthyste* in 1984. Each SNA has two crews. Maximum normal diving depth is reportedly 300 metres.

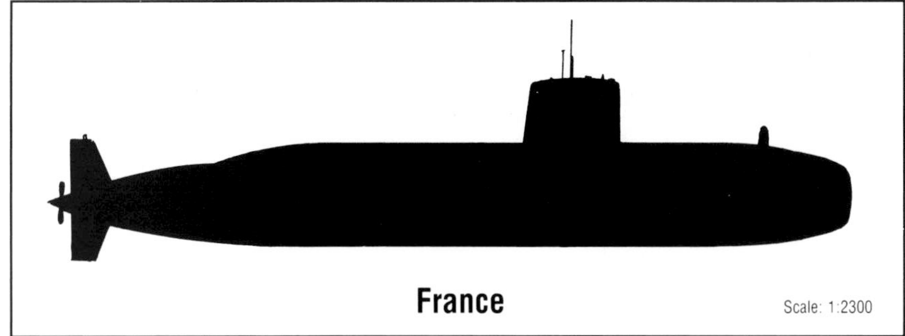

Photograph: *Rubis* 1985 (Naval Forces)

Trafalgar Class

Specifications and Technical Data

Number in class: 7

TRAFALGAR S107 1983
TURBULENT S87 1984
TIRELESS S88 1985
TORBAY S90 1987
TRENCHANT S91 1989
TALENT S92 1990
TRIUMPH S93 1991

Displacement, tonnes: 5,210 submerged
Dimensions, metres (feet): 85.4 × 9.8 × 8.5 (280.1 × 32.1 × 28)
Torpedo tubes: 5 × 533 mm forward
Sonar: 2026 or 2046 towed array, 2020 active/passive low-frequency hull array, 2007 hull-mounted passive medium/high-frequency flank array, 2019 passive/active ranging and intercept
Radar: 1006 I band navigation
Action Information Organisation: DCB
Machinery: 1 × PWR 1 pressurised water reactor, 2 × General Electric geared steam turbines, 1 × shaft, shrouded pump jet propulsor, 15,000 hp; diesel-battery electric emergency propulsion.
Speed, knots: 32
Range, nautical miles: limited only by endurance of crew, normally 85 days
Complement: 97

Photograph: *Tireless* 1986 (van Ginderen/USNI)

Trafalgar was completed with a normal propeller but the rest of the class were fitted with the shrouded pump jet for high, silent speed. The machinery is mounted on a raft suspended from transverse bulkheads: anechoic tiles further reduce noise both radiated and reflected. The reactor has a low speed natural circulation facility and a new longer life 'Z' core. The fin is strengthened and the forward hull-mounted hydroplanes are retractable in order to facilitate operations under the ice pack. Normal diving depth is about 300 metres, but the boats can reach around 600 metres maximum. About 20 Spearfish or Mk 24 Tigerfish dual purpose anti-submarine/anti-surface homing torpedoes or Sub-Harpoon anti-surface ship missiles are carried. Stonefish mines may be carried as alternatives. The 'Trafalgar' class submarines are allocated to the 2nd Submarine Squadron based at Devonport. Their major wartime role would be forward operations against Soviet submarines in their home waters. The 'Trafalgars' were all built by Vickers at Barrow-in-Furness. The first boat was ordered in 1977 and laid down in 1979 and the rest of the class ordered respectively in 1978, 1979, 1981, 1983, 1984 and 1986. The final boat seems to have been an additional unit as 1981 plans were for only 17 SSNs. Possibly extended refit times necessitated the additional boat in order to maintain operational numbers at sea. The 1007 radar will replace 1006.

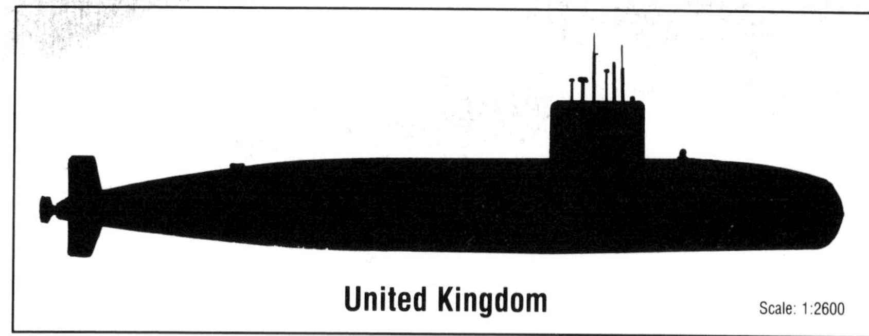

Specifications and Technical Data

Number in class: 6

SWIFTSURE S126 1973
SOVEREIGN S108 1974
SUPERB S109 1976
SCEPTRE S104 1978
SPARTAN S105 1979
SPLENDID S106 1981

Swiftsure Class

Displacement, tonnes: 4,500 submerged
Dimensions, metres (feet): 82.9 × 9.8 × 8.5 (272 × 32.3 × 28)
Torpedo tubes: 5 × 533 mm forward
Sonar: 2046 towed array, 2020 or 2001 active/passive low-frequency hull array, 2007 hull-mounted medium high-frequency passive flank array, 2019 passive/active ranging and interception
Radar: 1006 I band navigation
Action Information Organisation: DCB
Machinery: 1 × PWR1 pressurised water reactor, 2 × General Electric geared steam turbines, 1 × shaft, 15,000 hp, diesel electric-battery emergency propulsion
Speed, knots: over 30
Range, nautical miles: unlimited
Complement: 116

Ordered between 1967 and 1976, the 'Swiftsure' class was built to a new design emphasising high, very quiet performance for passive sonar anti-submarine operations. Almost all machinery is raft-mounted to reduce noise and the reactor runs on natural water circulation at low speeds. The machinery spaces are more compact than in older British SSNs and a small retractable auxiliary propulsion unit replaces the main electric motor of the 'Valiants'. The torpedo room is below the main decks beneath the fin and the tubes are angled from the centreline. Around 20 weapons are carried, Mk 24 Tigerfish or Spearfish homing torpedoes and Sub-Harpoon anti-ship missiles. All were originally fitted with the 2001 sonar, chin-mounted to reduce surface reflections but 2020 has been fitted in *Superb*, *Sceptre*, *Spartan* and *Splendid*. At least three of this class will receive 2074 sonar instead of 2020. Previously based at Devonport, these boats are to be transferred to the 3rd Submarine Squadron at Faslane in Scotland. The DCB action information system is based around two Ferranti 1600 B computers. The 'Swiftsure' class was built by Vickers at Barrow-in-Furness. *Swiftsure* was laid down in 1969 and launched in 1971, *Sovereign* was laid down in 1970 and launched in 1973, *Superb* was laid down in 1972 and launched in 1974, *Sceptre* was laid down in 1974 and launched in 1976, *Spartan* was laid down in 1976 and launched in 1978, and *Splendid* was laid down in 1977 and launched in 1979. *Splendid* and *Spartan* served in the Falklands War in 1982.

Photograph: *Swiftsure* 1989 (van Ginderen/USNI)

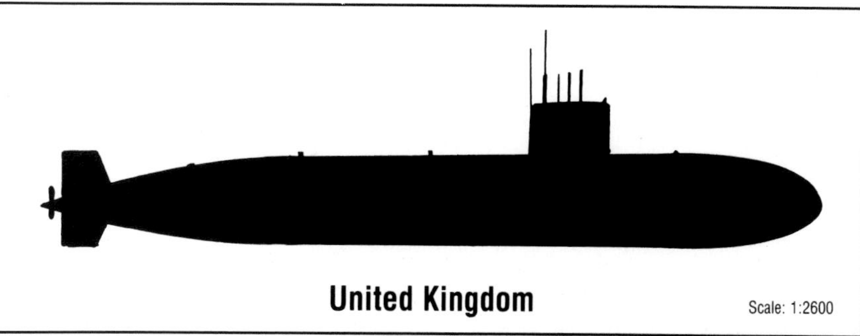

United Kingdom

Scale: 1:2600

Specifications and Technical Data

Number in class: 5

VALIANT S102 1966
WARSPITE S103 1967
CHURCHILL S46 1970
CONQUEROR S48 1971
COURAGEOUS S50 1971

Valiant Class

Displacement, tonnes: 4,900 submerged
Dimensions, metres (feet): 86.9 × 10.1 × 8.2 (285 × 33.2 × 27.5)
Torpedo tubes: 6 × 533 mm forward
Sonar: 2046 towed array, 2001 or 2020 hull-mounted active/passive low-frequency bow array, 2007 medium high-frequency passive flank array, 2019 passive/active ranging and intercept.
Radar: 1006 I band navigation
Action Information Organisation: DCA/DCB
Machinery: 1 × PWR1 pressurised water reactor, 2 × English Electric geared steam turbines, 15,000 hp, diesel/battery electric auxiliary propulsion
Speed, knots: 28
Range, nautical miles: limited only by endurance of crew
Complement: 116

HMS *Valiant* was the first all-British SSN as *Dreadnought* (currently awaiting final disposal at Rosyth), the first Royal Navy SSN in commission, used American machinery. *Valiant* was laid down in 1962 at Vickers, Barrow-in-Furness and launched on 3 December 1963 but her completion was delayed by difficulties with the new reactor and diversion of materials into the 'Resolution' class SSBNs. *Warspite* was laid down in 1963 and launched in 1965. *Churchill* was laid down in 1967 to a slightly modified design and was launched within eighteen months in 1968. *Conqueror* was the only British SSN not built by Vickers being constructed by Cammell Laird in Birkenhead. She was laid down in December 1967 and launched in August 1969. *Courageous* was laid down at Vickers in 1968 and launched in 1970. Modified sonar is being added to all but *Warspite* at refit and *Conqueror* was fitted with experimental 2075 sonar in 1987 for trials. She was the first nuclear submarine to sink an enemy warship, the Argentine cruiser *General Belgrano*, on 2 May 1982 using old Mk 8 torpedoes. The modern weapons load for the class is 26 Tigerfish or Spearfish anti-submarine and anti-surface homing torpedoes or Sub-Harpoon anti-ship missiles. The 'Valiant' class is operated by the 3rd Submarine Squadron out of Faslane. For their time they were quiet boats with 'raft-mounted' turbines and gearing but the electric auxiliary motor is used to achieve maximum quietness. The raft has to be locked at very high speeds. Diving depth is 230 m.

Photograph: *Conqueror* 1986 (van Ginderen/USNI)

Number in class: 2

CLEMENCEAU R98 1961
FOCH R99 1963

Specifications and Technical Data

Displacement, tonnes: 32,700 full load
Dimensions, metres (feet): 265 × 51.2 × 8.6 (869.4 × 168 × 28.2)
Aircraft: 16 × Super Étendard strike, 3 × Étendard IVP reconnaissance, 10 × Crusader fighters, 7 × Alizé ASW, 2 Alouette III helicopters
Missiles: SAM: 4 × 8 Crotale Navale, 36 missiles
Guns: 4 × 100mm, 2 × single mounts port side forward and starboard side aft
Sonar: SQS 505 medium-frequency hull-mounted active search
Radar: DRBV 23B D band air search, DRBI 10 E/F band air/surface search, DRBV 15 E/F band air/surface search, Decca 1226 I band navigation, DRBC 32C I band fire control, NRBA 51 landing approach control
Action Information Organisation: SENIT 2
Machinery: 2 × sets Parsons geared steam turbines, 2 × shafts, 126,000 hp, 6 × boilers
Speed, knots: 32
Range, nautical miles: 7,500 at 18 knots, 4,800 at 24 knots
Complement: 1,338

Light fleet carriers projected in the 1953 and 1955 budgets and the first aircraft carriers designed and built in France. *Clemenceau* was laid down at Brest Naval Dockyard in November 1955 and launched in December 1957. Foch was laid down at Chantiers de l'Atlantique at St. Nazaire in February 1957 and launched in July 1960. Both have been refitted to carry nuclear weapons and both have been fitted with SENIT 2 tactical data systems removed from old destroyers. The normal air group can be altered to suit both the mission and the availability of aircraft. There are only enough Crusader fighters for one air group and, if not in refit, the other carrier operates with a mix of Étendards and helicopters, or with up to 40 helicopters, e.g. a mixed air group might be made up of 17 helicopters, 10 Pumas, 4 Gazelles and 3 Super Frélons plus 10 Super Étendards and 4 Étendard IVPs. Each carrier is equipped with two BS5 steam catapults and the flight deck is angled at 8°. There are two 16 × 11 metre lifts and the 24 metre high hangar has a volume of 30,240 cubic metres. The hull over the machinery spaces and magazines. the flight deck and the superstructure is armoured. *Clemenceau* will be replaced in 1996 by the 36,000 ton nuclear-powered *Charles de Gaulle* laid down in 1989. *Foch* will remain in service until 2001 and a decision has not been taken on her replacement.

Photograph: *Clemenceau* 1987 (ECP Armées/USNI)

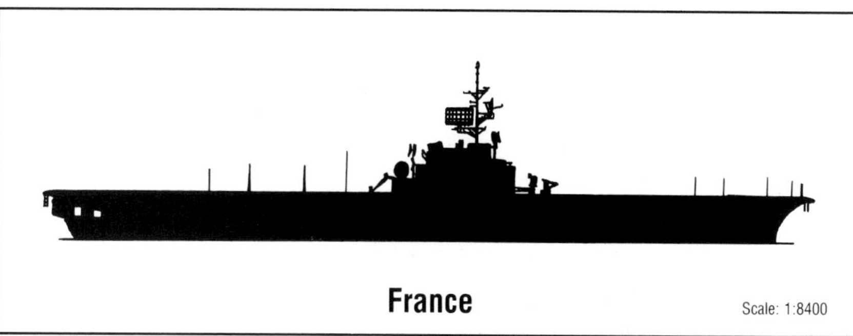

France

Scale: 1:8400

R97

Helicopter Carrier/Training Ship
Jeanne d'Arc Class

Number in class: 1

JEANNE d'ARC R97 1964

Specifications and Technical Data

Displacement, tonnes: 12,365 full load
Dimensions, metres (feet): 182 × 24 × 7.3 (597 × 78.7 × 24)
Aircraft: peacetime 6, e.g. 4 × Lynx and 2 × Alouette III; wartime 8 Super Frélons
Missiles: 2 × 3 MM 38 Exocet forward
Guns: 4 × 100mm, 2 single mounts forward and 2 aft
Sonar: DUBV 24 hull-mounted medium-frequency active
Radar: DRBV 22D D band air search, DRBV 50 G band air/surface search, DRBN 32 I band navigation, DRBC 32A I/J band fire control
Action Information Organisation: SENIT 2
Machinery: 2 × sets, Rateau-Bretagne geared steam turbines, 2 × shafts, 40,000 hp, 4 × boilers
Speed, knots: 26.5
Range, nautical miles: 5,500 at 20 knots, 3,000 at 26.5 knots
Complement: 627

Built primarily as a training cruiser for officer cadets, *Jeanne d'Arc* can be converted in an emergency into a multi-purpose ASW/amphibious assault helicopter carrier or troop transport. The PH57 design is based on that of the cruiser *Colbert*, but with reduced power. The 1,302 square metre flight deck has six helicopter spots and a 12 ton capacity elevator aft. Two small landing craft are also carried on davits amidships. It was originally intended that the ship should carry two extra 100 mm mountings abreast the superstructure. An ASW rocket launcher was to have been fitted but this never appeared and neither did the Masurca SAM launcher that was to have replaced it. The Exocet SSMs were mounted in 1974. On her annual six-month training cruises from Brest she carries 182 officers under training. Her maximum troop complement is about 700. The hangar deck is normally used partly as living quarters for the officer cadets, but this can be rapidly cleared to provide space for operational helicopters. Authorised in the budget of 1957 she was built at the Naval Dockyard, Brest, being laid down on 7 July 1960 and launched on 30 September 1961. She commissioned for trials on 16 July 1963 and entered service at the end of June 1964. Her original name was *La Résolue* as the old training cruiser *Jeanne d'Arc* was still in commission. She carries two eight-barrelled trainable chaff launchers for protection from missile attack. It is intended that *Jeanne d'Arc* will remain in service until 2004.

Photograph: *Jeanne d'Arc* 1988 (van Ginderen/USNI)

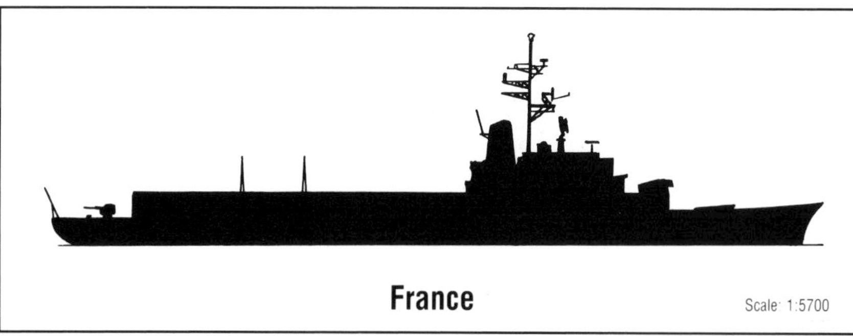

551

Number in class: 1

GIUSEPPE GARIBALDI C551 1987

Specifications and Technical Data

Displacement, tonnes: 13,240 full load
Dimensions, metres (feet): 180 × 33.4 × 6.7 (591 × 110.2 × 22)
Aircraft: 16 × SH-3D Sea King ASW helicopters or 10 × Harrier-type fighters and 5 × Sea Kings
Missiles: SSM: 4 × 1 Otomat Mk 2 aft
SAM: 2 × 8 Albatros with 48 Aspide missiles
Guns: 3 × 2 40mm, two mountings forward and one aft
Torpedoes: 6 × 324 mm for A224S ASW LWT
Sonar: DE 1160 LF medium-frequency bow-mounted active
Radar: SPS 52C 3D E/F band long range air search, RAN 3L D band air search, RAN 10S E/F band air/surface search, SPS 720 I band surface search/target indication, SPN 727 I band air control, SPN 703 I band navigation, RTN 30X SAM fire control, RTN 20X gun fire control
Action Information Organisation: IPN 20
Machinery: 4 × Fiat/General Electric LM 2500 gas turbines, 2 × shafts, 80,000 shp
Speed, knots: 30
Range, nautical miles: 7,000 at 20 knots
Complement: 780

Photograph: *Giuseppe Garibaldi* 1987 (USNI)

This is the first aircraft carrier completed by the Italian Navy. The contract for an improved helicopter cruiser was awarded in 1977 and the ship was laid down at Italcantieri at Monfalcone in 1981 and launched in June 1983. At the time the Italian Navy was legally debarred from operating fixed wing aircraft and this was only changed at the end of 1988. The ship, therefore, went to sea with an all helicopter air group but the Italian Navy has now been authorised to purchase up to eighteen fixed-wing aircraft, either EVA-8B Harrier II Plus or Sea Harrier FRS 2. The *Garibaldi* has a raised bow in order to provide a dry flight deck for helicopter operations in heavy weather but its major purpose, however, will be to provide a 6.5° ski-jump for the Harriers. The flight deck has two elevators, one forward and one aft and there are six spots for helicopter flight operations. The 9,900 cubic metre hangar can accommodate twelve Sea Kings with another four carried as a deck park. The *Garibaldi*'s primary role is the centrepiece of a multi-purpose 'Gruppo d'Altura' at least two of which are required in the Mediterranean. She is also the official flagship of the Italian Navy. She can carry two fast launches. A sister ship is projected. The DE 1160 LF sonar is the Raytheon commercially exported version of the US Navy's SQS 56 fitted with a larger, lower frequency transducer array and extra transmitter cabinets.

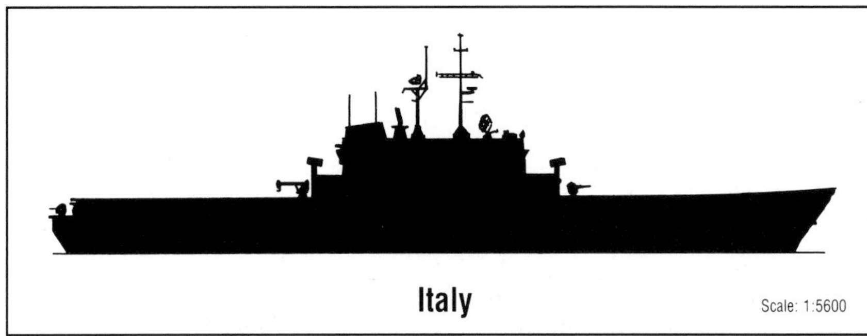

550
550

Number in class: 1

VITTORIO VENETO C550 1969

Helicopter-Carrying Cruiser
Vittorio Veneto Class

Specifications and Technical Data

Displacement, tonnes: 8,850 full load
Dimensions, metres (feet): 179.6 × 19.4 × 6 (589 × 63.6 × 19.7)
Aircraft: 9 × AB 212 ASW helicopters
Missiles: SSM: 4 × 1 Otomat Mk 2, two on each beam
SAM and ASW: 1 × twin Aster launcher forward with 40 Standard SM-1 ER and 20 ASROC
Guns: 8 × 1 76mm, four on each beam, 3 × 2 40mm, one forward and two aft
Torpedoes: 2 × 3 324 mm ASW for MK 46 LWT
Sonar: SQS 23G bow-mounted medium-frequency active
Radar: SPS 52C 3D E/F band long range air search, RAN 3L D band air search, SPS 702I band surface search/target indication, RM7 I band navigation, RTN 10X I/J band76 mm fire control, RTN 20X I/J band 40mm fire control, SPG 55C G/H band SAM fire control
Action Information Organisation: SADOC 1
Machinery: 2 × sets Tosi geared steam turbines, 2 × shafts, 73,000 shp, 4 × boilers
Speed, knots: 32
Range, nautical miles: 5,000 at 17 knots, 3,000 at 28 knots
Complement: 557

Vittorio Veneto was projected in the 1959-60 programme but like many Italian ships she was a long time in gestation. Originally intended to be a third 'Andrea Doria' the design was progressively enlarged until the *Veneto* was fifty per cent bigger. She was laid down at the Castellammare yard in June 1965 and launched in February 1967. *Veneto* has twice the helicopter complement of the 'Dorias' and provided a basis for the contemporary helicopter cruiser concept that was developed in Britain into a 'through-deck' aircraft carrier. The flight deck is 40 metres long and 18.5 metres wide and has two elevators leading into the hangar below. The small helicopters are stored on two decks. The ship received a major modernisation from 1981 to 1984 which added the Otomat missiles and the twin 40 mm guns, with new Italian fire control radar. Until the completion of the *Garibaldi* she was flagship of the Italian fleet and now provides the centrepiece of, and command ship for, the second 'Gruppo d'Altura' in the Mediterranean. She carries two 20-barrelled trainable chaff launchers to protect her from missile attack as well as an electronic intercept and jamming suite. The Augusta-Bell 212 helicopter carries an ASQ-18 dipping sonar and light-weight torpedoes or depth charges. It also carries a search/attack radar and can carry Sea Killer anti-ship missiles. The helicopter can also be used for electronic surveillance and countermeasures.

Photograph: *Vittorio Veneto* 1986 (USNI)

Italy

Scale: 1:5700

R11
R11

Number in class: 1

PRINCIPE DE ASTURIAS R11 1988

Aircraft Carrier Principe de Asturias Class

Specifications and Technical Data

Displacement, tonnes: 16,200 full load
Dimensions, metres (feet): 195.9 × 24.3 × 9.4 (642.7 × 79.7 × 30.8)
Aircraft: Up to 24, a mix of 6–12 × AV–8B and AV–8A (Harrier) STOVL fighters and 10–18 × helicopters. Sea King ASW and early warning and AB 212 ASW and surface search.
Guns: 4 Bazan Meroka 12-barrelled, 20 mm two forward, two aft.
Sonar: SPS 52C 3D E/F band air search, SPS 55 I/J band surface search, SPN 35A J band aircraft control, VPS 2 I/J band Meroka fire control
Action Information Organisation: Tritan NTDS
Machinery: 2 × General Electric LM 2500 gas turbines, 1 × shaft, 46,400 shp; 2 × 800 hp electric motors with retractable propeller for emergency propulsion
Speed, knots: 26
Range, nautical miles: 6,500 at 20 knots
Complement: 763

Photograph: *Principe de Asturias* (Naval Forces)

Based on the American Sea Control Ship concept of a light ASW helicopter carrier with a 12° 'ski-jump' added in order to facilitate the operation of STOVL fighters. Spain had operated AV-8A Matadors from the old ex-American carrier *Dedalo* since 1976 and acquired the improved AV-8B from the USA for her new ship. *Dedalo* has been withdrawn from service. The AV–8B 'Bronco' II aircraft are not yet fitted with radar although it is later intended to do so. A normal operational air group will be twenty aircraft, ten fighters and ten helicopters. *Principe de Asturias* is based at Rota but is intended for operations in the Atlantic as the core and flagship of 'Grupo Aeronavale Alfa', an ASW group. There are two lifts from the hangar to the flight deck, one right aft and the other forward of the superstructure. 208 of the ship's company are the flag officer's staff and the air group. The ship was ordered in June 1977 with the USA providing a substantial loan. She was laid down at the Bazan yard at Ferrol in 1979 and was launched in May 1982. Her completion was delayed by the addition of command facilities and changes in the command and control systems. The carrier has an American Prairie/Masker noise suppression system and tows the SLQ 25 Nixie torpedo decoy. Spain has three airborne early warning Sea King helicopters of which it is intended that two should be deployed in the carrier.

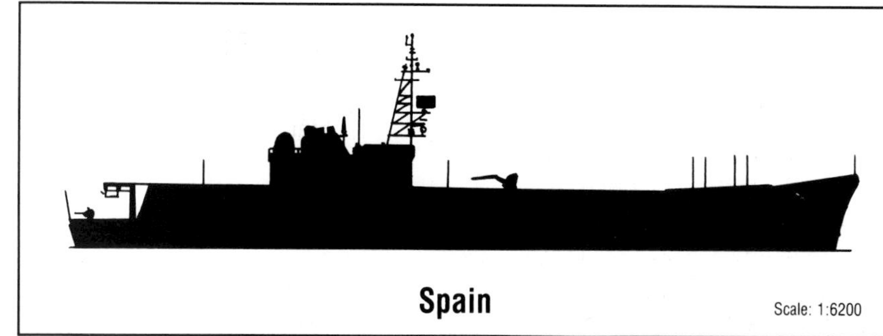

Spain

Scale: 1:6200

R06

Invincible Class

Number in class: 3

INVINCIBLE R05 1980
ILLUSTRIOUS R06 1982
ARK ROYAL R07 1985

Specifications and Technical Data

Displacement, tonnes: R05 and R06 19,960 full load, R07 20,600 full load
Dimensions, metres (feet): R05, R06 206.6 × 31.9 × 6.4 (677 × 105 × 21); R07 209.1 × 36 × 6.4 (685.8 × 118 × 21)
Aircraft: up to 9 × Sea Harrier STOVL fighters, up to 9 × Sea King ASW helicopters, 3 × Sea King AEW helicopters.
Missiles: SAM: 1 × twin Sea Dart launcher forward
Guns: R05 3 × 30 mm Goalkeeper CIWS; R06 2 × 20 mm Vulcan Phalanx CIWS; R07 3 × Vulcan Phalanx CIWS; 2 × 1 20 mm in all; 2 × twin 30 mm in R07
Sonar: R07 2016 hull-mounted medium frequency active
Radar: 1022 D band air search, 992R E/F band surface search, 1006 I band navigation, 909 I/J band fire control
Action Information Organisation: ADAWS 5
Machinery: 4 × Rolls-Royce Olympus TM3B gas turbines, 2 × shafts, 112,000 shp
Speed, knots: 28
Range, nautical miles: 5,000 at 18 knots
Complement: 1,008

Originally conceived in the early 1960s as command cruisers able to carry large ASW helicopters, these ships acquired extra significance with the 1966 British decision not to build fleet carriers. By 1970 they had become 'Through Deck Command Cruisers' to operate Sea King helicopters. The first, HMS *Invincible*, was laid down at Vickers in Barrow on 20 July 1973. In 1975 the Labour Government announced the procurement of Sea Harrier STOVL fighters for the ship and plans to construct two more. *Illustrious* was laid down on 7 October 1976 and *Ark Royal* on 14 December 1978 both at Swan Hunter, Wallsend. By the time the ships were commissioned they had been officially redesignated CVS (anti-submarine aircraft carriers). More recently this has been changed to CVSA (A for attack) in recognition of the combat capability of the embarked Sea Harriers. These can carry out nuclear strike missions if required, although their major role is combat air patrol. The Sea Harriers can also carry out anti-ship missions with Sea Eagle missiles. The main role of the CVSAs is to act as the command ships of the two main components of the NATO Striking Fleet's ASW Striking Force. *Ark Royal* was built with a 12° ski-jump and *Invincible* had one added in her 1986-88 refit. *Illustrious* has a 7° ski-jump and will retain this until her refit due to start in 1991. Until then she will be in reserve as there are only air groups for two ships. She will also receive lightweight Seawolf point defence missiles.

Photograph: *Illustrious* (fore) and *Ark Royal* (Royal Navy)

A135
ARGUS

Number in class: 1

ARGUS A135 1988

Argus Class

Specifications and Technical Data

Displacement, tonnes: 28,163 full load
Dimensions, metres (feet): 175.1 × 30.4 × 8.2 (574.5 × 99.7 × 27)
Aircraft: 6 × Sea King helicopters
Guns: 2 × 2 30 mm, 1 × 2 20 mm
Radar: 1006 I band air/surface search, 994 I band navigation
Action Information Organisation: CANE
Machinery: 2 × Lindholmen-Pielstick 18PC2.5 diesels, 2 × shafts, 23,000 shp
Speed, knots: 19
Range, nautical miles: 20,000 at 19 knots
Complement: 254

Argus is the former container ship *Contender Bezant* built at C.N.R. Breda, Venice in 1981. She was chartered as an aviation transport during the Falklands War and was purchased in 1984 for conversion at Harland and Wolff, Belfast into an aviation training ship to replace *Engadine*. The conversion included the provision of extra accommodation which has been added in a large forward superstructure rather than inside a redesigned hull. This precluded fitting the ship with a through deck. The large flight deck, 113.5 metres long and 28 metres wide, was thickened to 1.9 metres with concrete for stability reasons. There are two elevators, one amidships and one abaft the funnel on the starboard side. The ship is normally used in the English Channel to train helicopter crews in operating procedures at sea. She is officially a merchantman being operated by the Royal Fleet Auxiliary and registered at Belfast. 79 of her crew are RFA and 38 RN plus 137 RN training staff and students. *Argus* carries 3,500 tons of fuel for transfer to other ships.

Photograph: *Argus* (HM Steele)

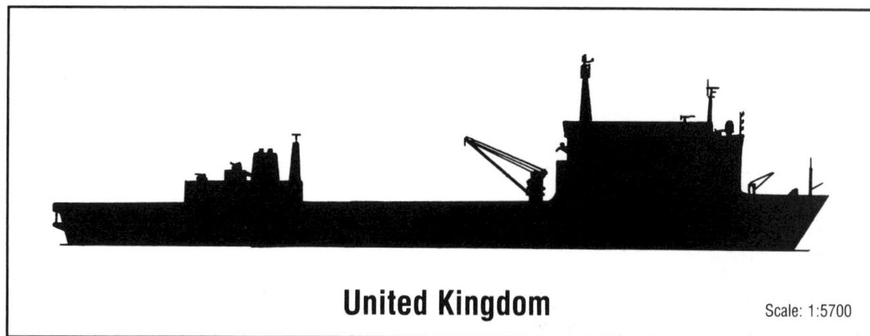

United Kingdom

Scale: 1:5700

F910

Specifications and Technical Data

Number in class: 4

WIELINGEN F910 1978
WESTDIEP F911 1978
WANDELAAR F912 1978
WESTHINDER F913 1978

Wielingen Class (Type E71)

Displacement, tonnes: 2,340 full load
Dimensions, metres (feet): 106.6 × 12.3 × 5.6 (349 × 40.3 × 18.4)
Missiles: SSM: 2 × 2 MM 38 Exocet aft
SAM: 1 × 8 Sea Sparrow aft
Guns: 1 × 100 mm forward
Torpedoes: 2 × 533 mm launchers for L5 HWT
ASW Weapons: 1 × 6 375 mm rocket launcher forward
Sonar: SQS 550A hull-mounted medium frequency active
Radar: DA 05 E/F band air/surface search, WM 25 I/J band surface search/fire control, TM 1645/9X I/J band navigation
Action Information Organisation: SEWACO IV
Machinery: 1 × Rolls-Royce Olympus TM3B gas turbine, 28,000 hp, 2 × Cockerill CO-240 V12 diesels, 6,000 hp, twin shafts
Speed, knots: 25
Range, nautical miles: 6,000 at 15 knots, 4,500 at 18 knots
Complement: 160

Until the 1970s Belgium concentrated on a mine countermeasures fleet, but in 1971 the construction of four small frigates was approved. After a two-year design process, orders were placed with Boelwerf of Temse and Cockerill of Hoboken for two ships each, **F910/912** and **911/913** respectively. *Vielengen* was laid down on 5 March 1974 and launched on 30 March 1976, *Vestdiep* was laid down on 2 September 1974 and launched on 8 December 1975, *Vandelaar* was laid down on 28 March 1975 and launched on 21 June 1977 and *Westhinder* was laid down on 8 December 1975 and launched on 28 January 1977. The first two ships were completed by the end of 1976 but suffered engine problems which delayed their commissioning until January 1978. The second pair were both commissioned on 27 October of that year. The ships are normally based at Zeebrugge, but are often seen at Den Helder working in close co-operation with the Dutch Navy. The ships are designed for Channel and North Sea operations but they also allow Belgium to make a contribution to NATO's Standing Force Atlantic (SNFL). Plans to fit the Goalkeeper close-in weapon system (CIWS) have not been put into effect. The original ASW torpedo launching racks are to be replaced by a new more conventional lightweight torpedo system. The maximum speed on diesel propulsion is 20 knots. Current maximum speed is reduced by 3-4 knots over the original trials speed.

Photograph: *Wielingen* (Belgian Navy)

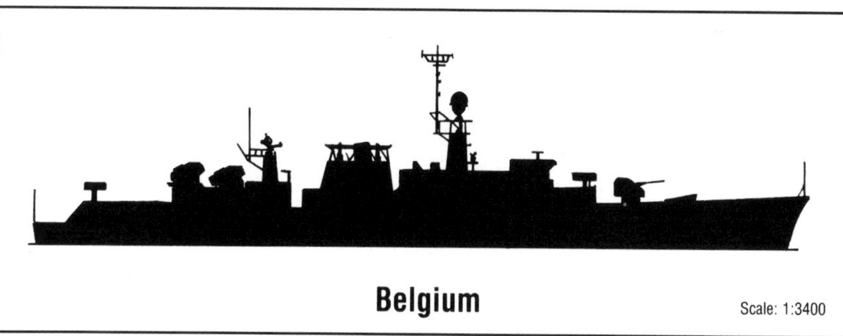

F352
F352

Number in class: 2

PEDER SKRAM F352 1966
HERLUF TROLLE F353 1967

Specifications and Technical Data

Displacement, tonnes: 2,720 full load
Dimensions, metres (feet): 112.6 × 12 × 3.6 (396.5 × 39.5 × 11.8)
Missiles: SSM: 2 × 4 Harpoon forward
SAM: 1 × 8 Sea Sparrow aft, 16 missiles
Guns: 1 × 2 127 mm forward, 4 × 1 40 mm, 4 × 1 20 mm
Torpedoes: 4 × 1 533 mm for Type 61 HWT
ASW Weapons: Depth charge rack
Sonar: PMS 26 hull-mounted active
Radar: CWS 2 and CWS 3 E/F band air/surface search, CGS 1 I band fire control, NWS 1 I band fire control, Skanter 009 E/I band navigation
Action Information Organisation: EPLO
Machinery: 2 × Pratt and Whitney PWA GG 4A-3 gas turbines, 44,000 hp, 2 × General Motors 16-567D diesels, 4,800 hp
Speed, knots: 28
Complement: 191

These two destroyer-like fast frigates were built to a Danish design by Helsingors J. and M. with American funds. **F352** was laid down on 25 September 1964 and launched on 20 May 1965 and **F353** was laid down on 18 December 1964 and launched on 8 September 1965. The frigates were modernised in 1977-78 with Harpoon and Sea Sparrow missiles and a modern computerised action information organisation. They were paid off into reserve in 1987 and are kept side by side with maintenance crews at Copenhagen. Maximum speed on diesel propulsion is 16 knots. The long-range heavyweight torpedoes are of Swedish design. Powered by hydrogen peroxide they are wire-guided and designed for use against surface targets. It is possible that Denmark may procure two more heavily-armed variants of the Stanflex 2000 patrol frigate as currently being constructed for fishery protection duties in order to replace the *Peder Skram*'s in the 1990s.

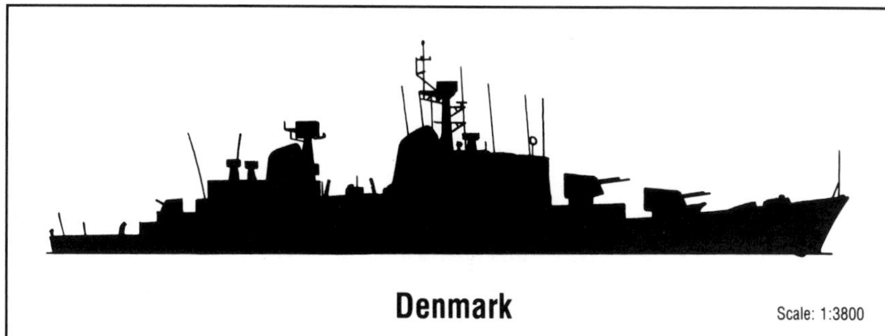

Photograph: *Peder Skram* 1986 (van Ginderen/USNI)

Nils Juel Class (Type KV72)

Number in class: 3

NILS JUEL F354 1980
OLFERT FISCHER F355 1981
PETER TORDENSKJOLD F356 1982

Specifications and Technical Data

Displacement, tonnes: 1,320 full load
Dimensions, metres (feet): 84 × 10.3 × 3.1 (275.5 × 33.8 × 10.2)
Missiles: SSM: 2 × 4 Harpoon amidships
SAM: 1 × 8 Sea Sparrow aft
Guns: 1 × 76 mm forward, 4 × 1 amidships
ASW Weapons: Depth charge rack at stern
Sonar: PMS 26 hull-mounted active
Radar: AWS 5 3D E/F band air search, 9GR 600 I band surface search, RTN 10 I/J band fire control, Scanter 009 E/I band navigation
Action Information Organisation: EPLO
Machinery: General Electric LM2500 gas turbine, 18,400 hp, MTU 20V956 TB82 diesel, 4,800 hp, two shafts
Speed, knots: 30
Range, nautical miles: 2,500 miles at 18 knots
Complement: 98

These small corvettes were designed by the Glasgow-based YARD design consultancy for general purpose duties in Danish waters. They were ordered at the end of 1975 and built by Aalborg Vaerft. **F354** was laid down on 20 October 1976 and launched on 17 February 1978, **F355** was laid down on 6 December 1976 and launched on 10 May 1979, and **F356** was laid down on 3 December 1979 and launched on 30 April 1980. Although designed in part for ASW operations they were not fitted with their planned ASW torpedo systems. They are thus primarily anti-surface warfare vessels for use in the Baltic Approaches in co-operation with Denmark's fleet of fast attack craft. No reloads are carried for the Sea Sparrow point defence system and this is due to be replaced by two launchers for General Dynamics RAM advanced anti-missile SAMs. Also to be added are two Italian SCLAR chaff/decoy rocket launchers for electronic countermeasures, although a Cutlass ESM is carried for radar warning. The computerised action information organisation is produced by DataSaab. The 76 mm gun is the OTO Melara 'compact' with a rate of fire of 85 rounds per minute. It has a range of 16 kilometres in the anti-surface mode. Maximum speed on diesels alone is 20 knots.

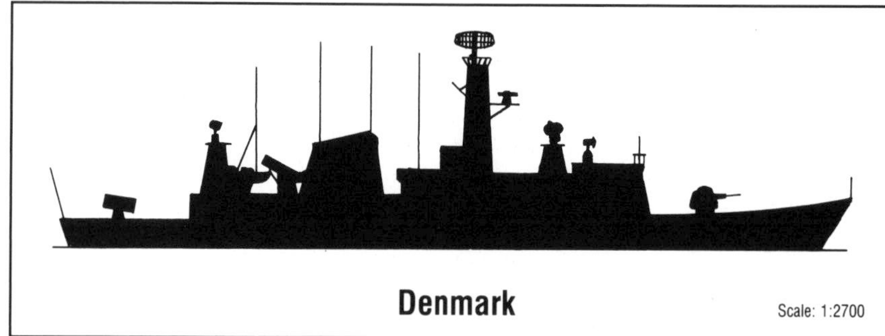

Denmark

Scale: 1:2700

Photograph: *Olfert Fischer* (Danish Navy)

F349
F349

Specifications and Technical Data

Number in class: 5

HVIDBJØRNEN F348 1962
VAEDDEREN F349 1963
INGOLF F350 1963
FYLLA F351 1963
BESKYTTEREN F340 1976

Hvidbjørnen, Modified Hvidbjørnen, Stanflex 2000 classes

Displacement, tonnes: 1,650; 1,970 full load
Dimensions, metres (feet): 72.6 × 11.6 × 5; 74.7 × 12.2 × 5.3 (238.2 × 38 × 16.4; 245 × 40 × 17.4)
Aircraft: 1 × Lynx helicopter
Guns: 1 × 76 mm forward
ASW Weapons: Depth charge racks
Sonar: PMS 26 hull-mounted active
Radar: AWS 6 G band air/surface search, Scanter 009 E/I band navigation
Machinery: 4 × General Motors 16-567C diesels, 640hp; 3 × Burmeister and Wain Alpha diesels, 7,440 hp, one shaft
Speed, knots: 18
Range, nautical miles: 6,000 at 13 knots
Complement: 82; 67

The first set of figures refers to **F348-351**, while the second set refers to **F340** which is 'Modified Hvidbjørnen' class. These ships carry NATO frigate pennant numbers but are coastguard vessels built for fishery protection duties in the North Sea and around the Faeroe Islands and Greenland where Denmark has extensive maritime policing responsibilities. Builders were Aalborg Vaerft (**F340**, **F349**, **F351**), Aarhus Flydedok (**F348**) and Svendborg Vaerft (**F350**). **F348** is modified for survey work and can carry survey launches instead of the helicopter. The four oldest ships are to be replaced by 2,700 ton (full load) Stanflex 2000 patrol frigates, four of which were ordered from Svendborg Vaerft in 1987 with the first laid down in 1988.

The dimensions of these new ships will be 104 × 14.4 × 6 metres (341.2 × 47.2 × 19.7 ft). Their 12,000 hp one shaft diesel electric propulsion system will give them a maximum speed of 20 knots and a range of 8,300 nautical miles at 18 knots. Unlike the older ships which carry old-style open mountings the new vessels will carry a rapid-fire 76 mm gun forward as well as one or two 20 mm weapons. A Lynx surveillance helicopter will be carried and sensors may be transferred from the older hulls. This much larger design could well form the basis of a more heavily-armed warship using the modularised equipment being developed for the Flex 300 fast attack craft. YARD have given design assistance with these ships.

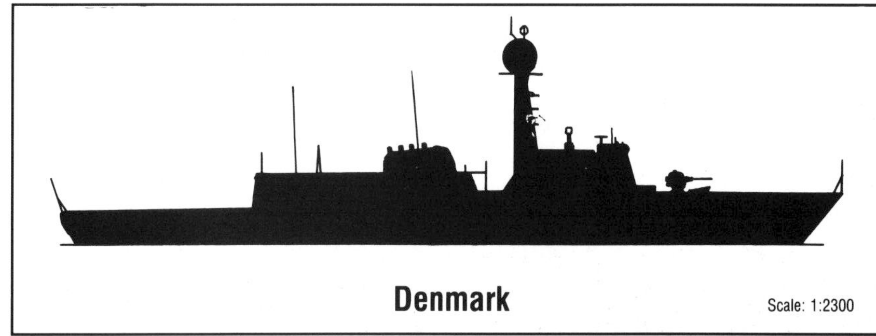

Denmark

Scale: 1:2300

Photograph: *Vaedderen* (Danish Navy)
Silhouette: Stanflex 2000

Number in class: 1

COLBERT C611 1959

Specifications and Technical Data

Displacement, tonnes: 11,300 full load
Dimensions, metres (feet): 180.8 × 20.2 × 7.7 (593.2 × 66.1 × 25.2)
Missiles: SSM: 4 × 1 MM 38 Exocet, 2 each side forward
SAM: 1 × 2 Masurca, 48 missiles
Guns: 2 × 1 100 mm forward, 6 × 2 57 mm, 3 on each beam amidships
Radar: DRBV 23C D band air search, DRBI 10D E/F band air search, DRBV 20C C band air search, DRBV 50 G band air/surface search, RM 416 I band navigation, DRBR 51 G/I band missile fire control, DRBR 32C I/J band 100 mm fire control, DRBC 31 I band 57 mm fire control
Action Information Organisation: SENIT 1
Machinery: 2 sets CEM Parsons geared steam turbines, 2 × shafts, 86,000 hp, 4 × boilers
Speed, knots: 31.5
Range, nautical miles: 4,000 at 25 knots
Complement: 560

Colbert was ordered as an anti-aircraft cruiser under the 1953 programme. She was built in Brest Naval Dockyard being started in 1954 and floated out of dry dock in March 1956. She began her trials in late 1957, finally commissioning on 5 May 1959. The design was an improved modification on that of the cruiser *De Grasse* laid down in 1938 but completed in 1956 as an AA ship. Eight twin 127 mm dual purpose guns were originally carried and ten twin 57 mm AA guns. In 1970 *Colbert* was taken in hand for a two and a half year rebuild as a guided missile armed command cruiser. This involved the fitting of new radar, the SENIT 1 computerised action information organisation, increased electrical power and improved habitability. As modified *Colbert* can act as the command ship for carrier task group or other tri-service operations. Normally, she is deployed as flagship of the Mediterranean Squadron based at Toulon. In 1981/82 she was refitted with an improved Masurca SAM system and Syracuse satellite communications. *Colbert* carries two 8-barrelled chaff launchers and jammers for electronic countermeasures and has an ARBR 10F radar warning ESM. A useful relic of her classic cruiser design is a 50-80 mm armoured belt and 50 mm deck protection. The machinery spaces are separated into two compartments each containing two boilers and a turbine. *Colbert* is expected to remain in service until 1997.

Photograph: *Colbert* (Naval Forces)

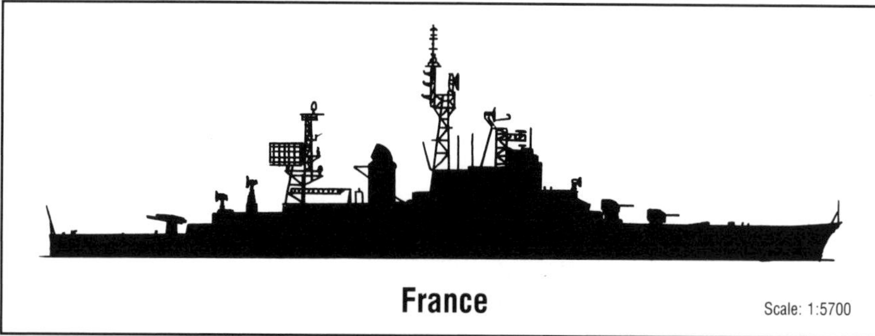

France

Scale: 1:5700

D614

Cassard (F70 A/A) Class

Number in class: 2

CASSARD D614 1988
JEAN BART D615 1991

Specifications and Technical Data

Displacement, tonnes: 4,340 full load
Dimensions, metres (feet): 139 × 14 × 5.7 (455.9 × 45.9 × 18.7)
Aircraft: 1 × Lynx helicopter
Missiles: SSM: 2 × 44 MM 40 Exocet amidships, 1 × 1 Standard SM-1 MR, 40 missiles, 2 × 6 Sadral point defence missile system
Guns: 1 × 10 mm forward, 2 × 1 20 mm in bridge wings
Torpedoes: 2 × fixed launchers for L5 ASW HWT
Sonar: DUBA 25A hull-mounted medium-frequency active
Radar: DRBV 15 E/F band air search, DRBV 26 D band air/surface search, Decca 1229 I band navigation, DRBC 33 I band fire control, SPG 51C G/I band Standard fire control
Action Information Organisation: SENIT 6
Machinery: 4 × SEMT-Pielstick 18PA6 V280 BTC diesels, 2 × shafts, 42,000 hp
Speed, knots: 29.5
Range, nautical miles: 8,000 at 17 knots, 4,800 at 24 knots
Complement: 240

Despite their NATO destroyer pennant numbers, these ships, like all 3,500-5,000 ton French fleet combatants, are classified as 'frégates'. Indeed until 1988 they, along with their anti-submarine cousins, were officially rated as 'corvettes'. There were to have been four anti-air F70s (formerly C70s) but the third and fourth ships, ordered in 1984, have been indefinitely postponed due to the unexpected non-availability of the American Standard SM-1 missile and the expense of the SM-2. The two Standard missile fits for these ships have been taken from old T-47 type destroyers, a sign of France's problems in funding its naval programmes. Both ships were laid down at the Naval Dockyard Lorient, *Cassard* on 3 September 1982 and *Jean Bart* on 12 March 1986. The ships were launched respectively on 6 February 1985 and 19 March 1988. The anti-air F70s have a totally different propulsion system from their ASW counterparts, being all diesel as opposed to the CODOG installation in the other ships. Building has been slow, the ships having been authorised as long ago as 1978/79. The Lynx helicopter is used primarily to help target the Exocet missiles and as a surface attack system in itself with AS12 missiles, but there is provision in the ship design for a DSBV 61A towed array to increase the emphasis on ASW. The DRBV 15 air search radar on *Cassard* is an interim fit until the DRBJ 11B 3D long-range air search radar becomes available.

Photograph: *Cassard* 1988 (David Smith/USNI)

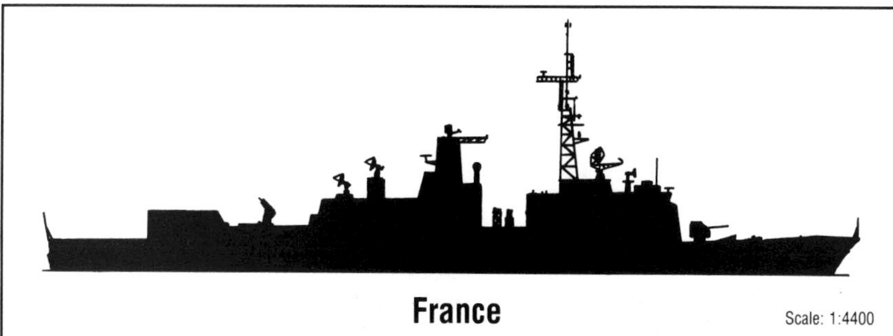

D645

Specifications and Technical Data

Number in class: 7

GEORGES LEYGUES D640 1979
DUPLEIX D641 1981
MONTCALM D642 1982
JEAN DE VIENNE D643 1984
PRIMAUGUET D644 1986
LA MOTTE-PICQUET D645 1988
LATOUCHE-TRÉVILLE D646 1990

Georges Leygues F70 (ASW) Class

Displacement, tonnes: 4,170 full load
Dimensions, metres (feet): 139 × 14 × 5.7 (455.9 × 45.9 × 18.7)
Aircraft: 2 × Lynx helicopters
Missiles: SSM: 4 × 1 (D640-1) MM 38, 2 × 4 (D642-6) MM 40 Exocet amidships.
SAM: 1 × 8 Crotale Navale aft, 26 missiles
Guns: 1 × 100 mm forward, 2 × 1 20 mm
Torpedoes: 2 launchers for L5 ASW HWT
Sonar: (D644-6) DSBV 61 towed array, (D640-3) DUVB 23D or (D644-6) DUBV 24C hull-mounted active, (D640-2) DUBV 43B or (D643-6) DUBV 43C medium-frequency variable depth
Radar: (D640-3) DRBV 26 D band air search and DRBV 51C G band air/surface search, (D644-6) DRBV 15A G band air/surface search, Decca 1226 I band navigation, (D640-3) DRBC 32D or (D644-6) DRBC 32E I/J band fire control
Action Information Organisation: SENIT 4
Machinery: 2 × Rolls-Royce Olympus gas turbines, 46,200 hp, 2 × SEMT-Pielstick 16PA6 CV280 diesels, 10,400 hp, 2 × shafts
Speed, knots: 30
Range, nautical miles: 8,500 at 18 knots
Complement: 216

Originally rated as 'Corvettes' and with destroyer pennant numbers these ASW ships were re-rated 'frégates' in 1988. Eight ships were originally projected but one has been cancelled. All seven were laid down in Brest Naval Dockyard, **D640** in 1974, **D641** and **D642** in 1975, **D643** in 1979, **D644** in 1981, **D645** in 1982 and **D646** in 1985 but the last two were towed to Lorient Naval Dockyard for completion. In the early 1990s towed array will be fitted to the first four members of the class which are currently deployed in the Mediterranean. The three towed array units, deployed in the Atlantic, have bridges raised by one deck. The range quoted in the table is on diesel power alone, at full power and maximum speed range is reduced to 1,000 nautical miles. Maximum speed on diesels alone is 21 knots. The helicopters are used both for ASW with torpedoes or depth charges and anti-surface ship attacks with AS12 missiles. Ten torpedoes are carried for the two launchers. From **D644** the Crotale EDIR system is fitted with modified fusing, infra-red tracker and increased range and all the F70 ASW frigates carry a gun for coastal bomardment.

Photograph: *La Motte-Picquet* 1987 (Jürg Kürsener/USNI)
Silhouette: D640-D643

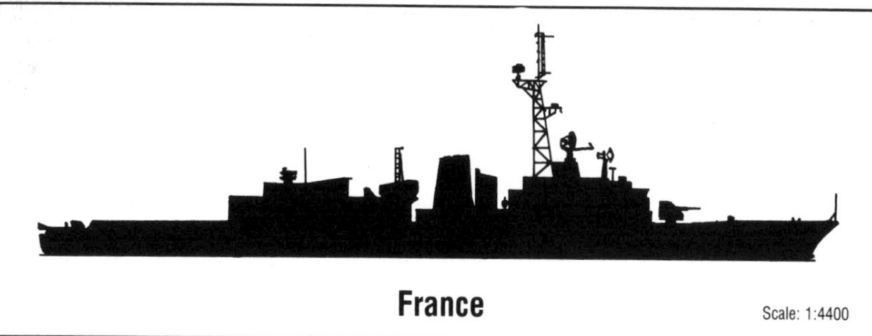

D612

Tourville (F67) Class

Number in class: 3

TOURVILLE D610 1974
DUGUAY-TROUIN D611 1975
DE GRASSE D612 1977

Specifications and Technical Data

Displacement, tonnes: 5,800 full load
Dimensions, metres (feet): 152.8 × 16 × 5.7 (501.6 × 52.4 × x18.7)
Aircraft: 2 × Lynx helicopters
Missiles: SSM: 6 × 1 MM 38 Exocet three on each beam abaft bridge
SAM: 1 × 8 Crotale Navale, 26 missiles.
ASW Weapons: Malafon
Guns: 2 × 1 100 mm forward, 2 × 1 20 mm in bridge wings
Torpedoes: 2 × launchers for L5 ASW HWT
Sonar: DUBV 61 towed array, DUBV 23 hull-mounted active, DUBV 43 medium-frequency variable depth
Radar: DRBV 26 D band air search, DRBV 51 G band air/ surface search, Decca 1226 I band navigation, DRBC 32D I/J band fire control
Action Information Organisation: SENIT 3
Machinery: 2 × Rateau geared steam turbines, 2 × shafts, 54,400 hp
Speed, knots: 32
Range, nautical miles: 4,5000 at 18 knots, 1,900 at 30 knots
Complement: 301

Developed as 5,000 ton C67A 'Corvettes' with 'F' pennant numbers for ASW duties, the ships were re-designated 'Frégates' and given 'D' numbers in 1971 before *Tourville* was launched. **D610** had been laid down in Lorient Naval Dockyard in March 1970. She was launched in May 1972. *Duguay-Trouin* was laid down at the same yard in February 1971 and *De Grasse* in June 1972. They were launched in June 1973 and November 1974 respectively. The 'F67s' are large and roomy with good seakeeping and a high standard of accommodation. *Duguay-Trouin* is fitted out as a flagship. Major modernisation of these ships is planned in the early 1990s. This will include a new combined hull-mounted and towed array VLF sonar system. This will confirm the 'F67s' as perhaps the most capable ASW units in the French Navy. They are expected to last in service until the early years of the next century. The ships' Crotale air defence missiles were fitted in 1979-81 and replaced a third 100 mm gun mounting aft. Twenty-six missiles are carried. The systems will be uprated with the EDIR modifications and the Syllex 8-barrelled trainable chaff launchers are to be replaced by two Dagaie systems. The helicopters double in the anti-submarine and anti-surface ship roles. The Malafon anti-submarine missile carries an L4 lightweight homing torpedo at 450 knots over a maximum range of 13 kilometres. Thirteen missiles are carried. Malafon is to be replaced by the improved Milas system.

Photograph: *De Grasse* (HM Steele/Naval Forces)

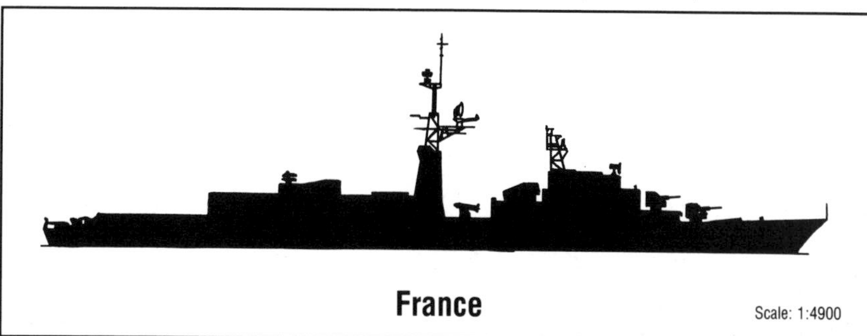

D609

Number in class: 1

ACONIT D609 1973

Anti-Submarine Frigate
Aconit (F65) Class

Specifications and Technical Data

Displacement, tonnes: 3.840
Dimensions, metres (feet): 127 × 13.4 × 5.5 (416.7 × 44 × 18.9)
Missiles: SSM: 2 × 4 MM 40 Exocet forward
ASW Weapons: 1 × Malafon launcher amidships, 13 missiles
Guns: 2 × 1 100 mm, 1 forward, 1 aft
Torpedoes: 2 × launchers for L5 ASW HWT
Sonar: DUBV 23 hull-mounted active, DUBV 43 medium-frequency variable depth
Radar: DRBV 22A D band air search, DRBV 15 E/F band air/surface search, DRBN 32 I band navigation, DRBC 32B I/J band 100 mm fire control
Action Information Organisation: SENIT 3
Machinery: 1 × Rateau geared steam turbine, 1 × shaft, 28,650 hp
Speed, knots: 27
Range, nautical miles: 5,000 at 18 knots
Complement: 228

Photograph: *Aconit* 1989 (van Ginderen/USNI)

Projected in the 1965 programme as the first of five anti-submarine 'Corvettes', *Aconit* was laid down at Lorient Naval Dockyard in January 1966 and launched on 7 March 1970. Even while under construction, however, it was decided that she was too small and the follow-on F67 ships were built in smaller numbers to a much larger twin screw design with provision for helicopters. *Aconit* has, therefore, remained unique although she serves as a front line unit with the Atlantic Squadron based at Brest. She is due to leave service at the end of the century, but it is planned to fit her with towed array sonar to enhance her ASW utility in the 1990s. The propulsion unit produced 31,500 hp on trials. The Exocet missiles were fitted on the forecastle in place of an anti-submarine mortar during her 1984-5 refit. Ten L5 ASW missiles are carried for the torpedo launchers. These large 1,000 kilogram weapons carry a 150 kilogram warhead at 35 knots out to 17 kilometres and down to depths of over 550 metres. The electronic warfare suite comprises an ARBR 16 radar warning ESM, an ARBB 32 jammer, two Syllex 8-barrelled chaff launchers and a Nixie towed torpedo decoy.

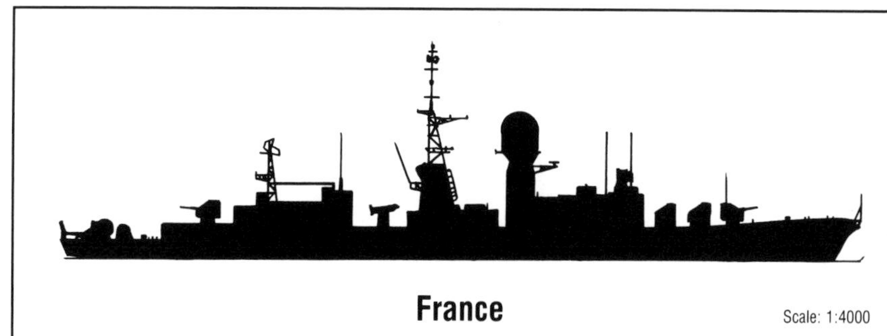

D602

Suffren Class

Number in class: 2

SUFFREN D602 1967
DUQUESNE D603 1970

Specifications and Technical Data

Displacement, tonnes: 6,090
Dimensions, metres (feet): 157.6 × 15.5 × 6.1 (517.1 × 50.9 × 20)
Missiles: SSM: 4 × 1 MM 38 Exocet aft
SAM: 1 × 2 Masurca aft, 48 missiles
ASW Weapons: Malafon launcher amidships, 13 missiles
Guns: 2 × 1 100 mm forward, 4 × 1 20 mm
Torpedoes: 4 × launchers for L5 ASW HWT
Sonar: DUBV 23 hull-mounted active, DUBV medium-frequency variable depth
Radar: DRBI 23 D band air search, DRBV 15 (D603) E/F band or DRBV 50 (D602) G band air/surface search, DRBN 32 I band navigation, DRBR 51 G/I band Masurca fire control, DRBC 32A I/J band 100 mm fire control
Action Information Organisation: SENIT 1
Machinery: 2 × sets Rateau geared steam turbines, 2 × shafts, 72,000 hp, 4 × boilers
Speed, knots: 34
Range, nautical miles: 2,400 at 29 knots, 5,100 at 18 knots
Complement: 355

Photograph: *Suffren* (ECP Armées/Naval Forces)

These large fleet destroyer-type ships were constructed as small escort cruisers to escort the French Navy's carriers, a task they still generally fulfil. Classified 'frégates' on entry into service *Suffren* and *Duquesne* were to have been joined by two sister ships but these were never built. Along with the carriers they are based at Toulon in the Mediterranean and both deployed to the Gulf during the Iran-Iraq war. Projected under the 1960-65 new construction programme Suffren was laid down at Lorient Naval Dockyard at the end of 1962 and launched on 15 May 1965. *Duquesne* was laid down in November 1964 at Brest and launched on 12 February 1966. Exocet was fitted in the late 1970s and improved Masurca in 1984-5. Other than their prominent 'Macks', their distinctive feature is their large radome covering the DRBI 23 air search radar. Their major weapon system is the Masurca Mk 2 missile with a range of 55 kilometres. A mix of beam riding and semi-active homing missiles is carried. The ships' ECM suite which includes an ARBB 32 jammer is being upgraded with Sagei and Dagei trainable chaff and flare launchers replacing the Syllex 8-barrelled trainable chaff launchers.

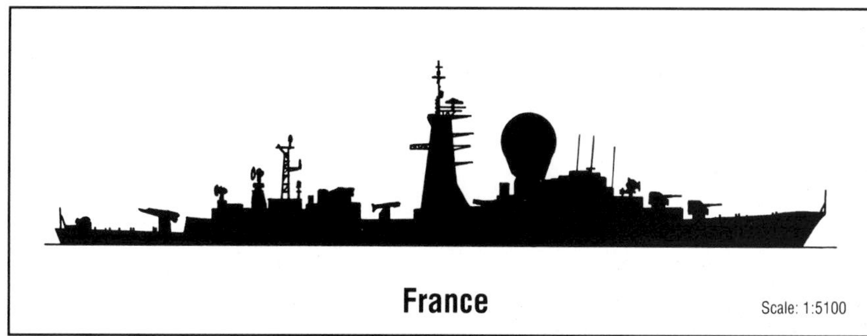

France

Scale: 1:5100

630
D630

Types T47, T53, T56

Number in class: 3

T47 DU CHAYLA D630 1957
T53 DUPERRÉ D633 1957
T56 LA GALISSONNIÈRE D638 1962

Specifications and Technical Data

Displacement, tonnes: 3,740 full load
Dimensions, metres (feet): 128.5(T47) 132.8(T53/56) × 12.7 × 6.3 (421.6 or 435.7 × 41.7 × 21.4)
Aircraft: (T53) 1 × Lynx, (T56) 1 × Alouette helicopter
Missiles: SAM: (T47) 1 × Standard SM1 MR launcher, 40 missiles
SSM: (T53) 4 × 1 MM 38 Exocet amidships,
ASW: (T56) 1 Malafon launcher aft, 13 missiles
Guns: (T47) 3 × 2 57 mm, (T53) 1 × 1 100 mm, (T56) 2 × 1 100 mm
Torpedoes: (T47/56) 2 × 3 550 mm for L3 ASW HWT (T53) 2 launchers for L5 ASW HWT
ASW Weapons: (T47) 1 × 6 375 mm rocket launcher forward
Sonar: (T47) DUBV 24 hull-mounted active, DUBA 1 active attack; (T53/56) DUBV23 hull-mounted active, DUBV43 medium-frequency variable depth
Radar: (T47) DRBV22 and SPS39 air search, DRBV31 surface search, SPG51B missile fire control, DRBC31 gun fire control; (T53) DRBV22A air search, DRBV51 air/surface search, Decca I band navigation, DRBC32E fire control; (T56) DRBV 22 air search, DRBV50 air/surface search, DRBN32 navigation, DRBC32A fire control
Action Information Organisation: SENIT 2
Machinery: 2 × Rateau geared steam turbines, 63,000 hp, 4 × boilers
Speed, knots: 32
Range, nautical miles: 5,000 at 18 knots
Complement: 270-7
Photograph: *Du Chayla* 1989 (David Smith/USNI)
Silhouette: *Duperré*

France's standard 'Surcouf' class fleet destroyer hull of the 1950s was converted into a number of different forms three of which are still in service although it unlikely that any will remain beyond 1990. *Du Chayla*, laid down at Brest Naval Dockyard in 1953 is one of the four original T47s converted in the early 1960s into a 'guided-missile squadron escort' carrying the American Tartar/Standard SAM system. Two of her sisters were withdrawn in 1982-3 to provide missile systems for the two F70 AA frigates. A third paid off into reserve in 1988 and **D630** will be replaced when *Jean Bart* enters service.
Duperré, laid down at Lorient in 1954, launched in 1956 and completed as a T53 radar picket was converted first into an unarmed sonar trials ship and then into an ASW flagship in 1972-4. *Duperré* was flagship of the Atlantic squadron, but was badly damaged in a grounding in 1978. She was repaired using parts cannibalised from her sister *Jaureguiberry*. *Duperré* was worth saving as she has virtually the capability of an F70 frigate except for air-defence missiles and the second Lynx.
La Galissonnière was laid down at Lorient in November 1958 and launched in 1960. She was the last of the 'Surcouf' line, a unique experimental vessel for ASW sensors and weapons. As such she was the first ship to carry the Malafon anti-submarine missile. She has an interesting helicopter arrangement for her ASW Alouette in which the hangar walls swing outwards in order to create a flight deck.

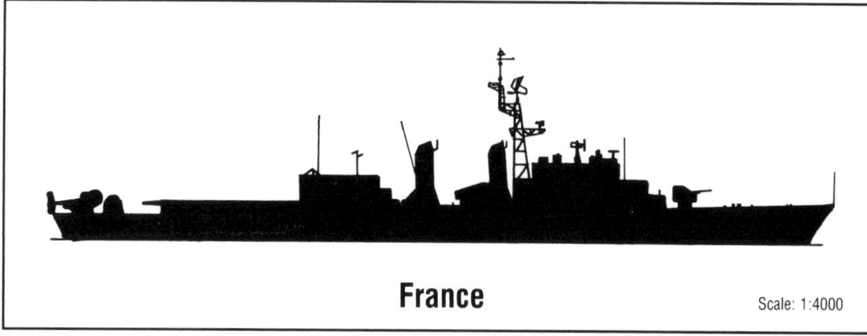

France

Scale: 1:4000

F730
FLOREAL

Floréal Class

Number in class: 2

FLORÉAL F800 1990
PRAIRIAL F801 1991

Specifications and Technical Data

Displacement, tonnes: 2,850
Dimensions, metres (feet): 93.5 × 14 × 4.3 (306.8 × 45.9 × 14.1)
Aircraft: 1 × Super Puma helicopter
Missiles: SSM: 2 × 2 MM 40 Exocet amidships
SAM: 2 × 6 Sadral point defence launchers
Guns: 1 × 100 mm forward, 2 × 1 20 mm abaft bridge
Radar: DRBV 15 E/F band air/surface search, Decca 1226 I band navigation
Machinery: 4 × diesels, 2 × shafts, 8,000 hp
Speed, knots: 20
Range, nautical miles: 9,000 at 15 knots
Complement: 100

Six 'Frégates de Surveillance' were ordered in April 1988 from the Chantiers de l'Atlantique at St. Nazaire and the first pair are due in service in 1990-91 with the following four coming into service by 1993. The ships will be fitted out at Lorient Naval Dockyard by 1993. These are very basic units indeed, built to mercantile marine standards for presence, constabulary and gunboat duties both in France's offshore zone and among her far-flung colonial possessions. The ships have deliberately been given absolute minimal capabilities and can only engage submarines with a suitable helicopter. They can, however, report what is going on in the air or on the surface, deliver a small bombardment and land up to 24 marines by helicopter. The ships are intended to replace the old, 'Commandant Rivière' class sloops (Avisos) which are about to be taken out of service. France hopes to build in the mid to late 1990s larger fully combatant diesel-powered 3,200 ton light frigates. Eight were ordered in April 1988 but the first will not commission until 1994. These ships will have a hull-mounted active sonar, air/surface search radar, a small helicopter, Exocet and Crotale missiles and 100 mm gun. They are also intended for service in distant waters to replace the A69 sloops (Avisos).

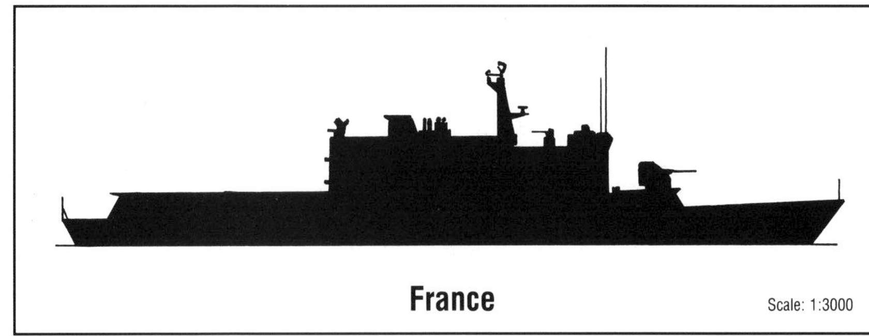

Photograph: Builders' model (Chantiers de l'Atlantique/Naval Forces)

Number in class: 17

D'ESTIENNE D'ORVES F781 1976
AMYOT D'INVILLE F782 1976
DROGOU F783 1976
DÉTROYAT F784 1977
JEAN MOULIN F785 1977
QUARTIER-MAÎTRE ANQUETIL F786 1978
COMMANDANT DE PIMODAN F787 1978
SECOND MAÎTRE LE BIHAN F788 1979
LIEUTENANT DE VAISSEAU LE HENAFF F789 1980
LIEUTENANT DE VAISSEAU LAVALLÉE F790 1980
COMMANDANT L'HERMINIER F791 1986
PREMIER MAÎTRE L'HER F792 1981
COMMANDANT BLAISON F793 1982
ENSEIGNE DE VAISSEAU JACOUBET F794 1982
COMMANDANT DUCUING F795 1983
COMMANDANT BIROT F796 1984
COMMANDANT BOUAN F797 1984

D'Estienne d'Orves (A69) Class

Displacement, tonnes: 1,250
Dimensions, metres (feet): 80 × 10.3 × 5.5 (262.5 × 32.8 × 18)
Missiles: SSM: (F792-7) 2 × 2 MM 40 Exocet (F781, 783,786-7) 2 MM 38 Exocet amidships
Guns: 1 × 100 mm forward, 2 × 1 20 mm amidships
Torpedoes: 4 × fixed tubes for L3 (refitted units L5) ASW HWT
ASW Weapons: 1 × 6 375 mm rocket launcher aft
Sonar: DUBA 25 hull-mounted medium-frequency
Radar: DRBV 51A G band air/surface search, Decca 1226 I band navigation, DRBC 32E I/J band fire control
Machinery: 2 × SEMT-Pielstick 12PC2 V400 (F791 12PA6BTC) diesels, 2 × shafts, 12,000 hp (F791 14,400hp)
Speed, knots: 23
Range, nautical miles: 4,500 at 15 knots
Complement: 92

Photograph: *Commandant Ducuing* (DCN/Naval Forces)

A large class of 'Avisos' or sloops designed for foreign presence and coastal escort operations. Maximum endurance of the class is 15 days. They can carry a small marine detachment of eighteen men. They are deployed in five divisions, each of three to four ships, the 1st at Cherbourg, the 2nd and 4th at Brest and the 3rd and 5th at Toulon. The four MM 38 Exocet equipped ships are deployed in the Mediterranean. The ships are very small and plans to fit a helicopter to two of the last units were abandoned. One ship carried out trials with a Crotale SAM launcher in place of the forward gun in 1986, but lack of AA armament remains a serious problem with the type. The last seven ships were fitted with Dagaie chaff launchers. *Amyot d'Inville* was the first to be refitted in 1986 with a modified gun, upgraded sonar, Dagaie launchers, Nixie torpedo decoy and L5 ASW torpedoes. **F791** was fitted with the new engines as a trials ship for the F70 AA frigates. She has special features to suppress her infra-red signature. The class will be withdrawn from service between 1996 and 2004. All were built at Lorient Naval Dockyard, the first being laid down in September 1972 and launched in June 1973 and the last being laid down in October 1981 and launched in April 1983.

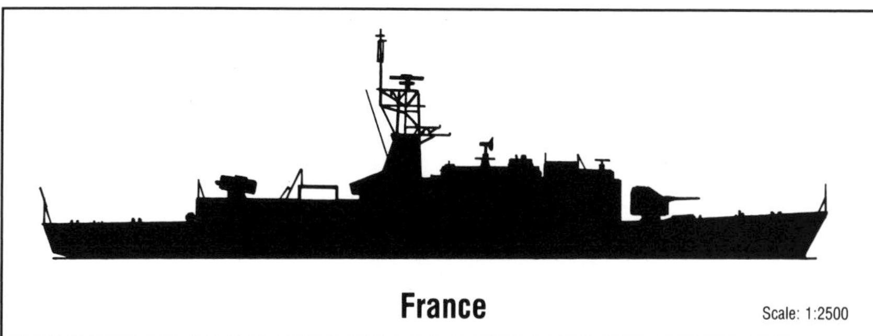

France

Scale: 1:2500

Commandant Rivière Class

Specifications and Technical Data

Number in class: 7

COMMANDANT BORY F726 1964
AMIRAL CHARNER F727 1962
DOUDART DE LAGRÉE F728 1963
BALNY F729 1970
COMMANDANT BOURDAIS F740 1963
PROTET F748 1964
ENSEIGNE DE VAISSEAU HENRY F749 1965

Displacement, tonnes: 2,230
Dimensions, metres (feet): 102.7 × 11.7 × 4.3 (336.9 × 38.4 × 14.1)
Missiles: SSM: (except F729) 4 × 1 MM 38 Exocet aft
Guns: 2 × 1 100 mm, 1 forward, 1 aft, 2 × 1 30 mm (F729, 748, 749) or (rest) 40 mm amidships
Torpedoes: 2 × 3 550 mm for L3 ASW HWT
ASW Weapons: 1 × 305 mm quadruple mortar
Sonar: SQS 17 hull-mounted medium-frequency active search, DUBA 3 active attack
Radar: DRBV 22A D band air/surfce search, Decc 1226 I band navigation, DRBC 32C I/J band fire control
Machinery: 4 × SEMT-Pielstick 12PC diesels, 16,000 hp, 2 × shafts, (F729, 2 × Turbomeca M38 gas turbine and 2 × AGO V16 diesels, 18,700 hp, 1 × shaft)
Speed, knots: 26
Range, nautical miles: 7,500 at 16.5 knots, (F729, 13,000 at 10 knots)
Complement: 166 (F729, 169)

Six of these Avisos are based overseas, three in the Pacific and three in the Indian Ocean. **F740** operates as a training ship in the Atlantic. A sister ship was sold to Uruguay in 1988 and the name ship of the class was converted to a sonar trials ship in 1985. Although used operationally, **F729** *Balny* was chosen to be the French Navy's CODAG trials ship. Although completed in 1964 she did not commission for another six years. She can carry more fuel than her sisters which gives her greater range. *Balny* carries her after gun on top of the superstructure which means that she is unable to ship Exocet missiles. She will, however, be the last of the class in service, being scheduled for withdrawal in 1994. The ASW mortar has a range of up to 3 kilometres with a 230 kilogram projectile. It can also be used with 100 kilogram projectile against land targets up to 6 kilometres away. Up to 80 troops can be carried together with two small landing craft. The ships were built at Lorient Naval Dockyard. The seven survivors were laid down between 1958 and 1962. Launch dates were: **F726** October 1958, **F727** March 1960, **F728** April 1961, **F719** March 1962, **F740** April 1961, **F748** December 1962, **F749** December 1963. They have been the backbone of France's foreign naval presence for many years and will be replaced by he new, but much less capable, 'Frégates de Surveillance'.

Photograph: *Commandant Bory* (Naval Forces)

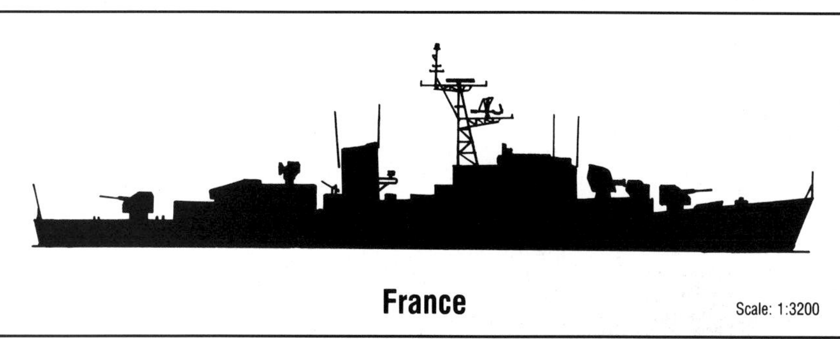

France

Scale: 1:3200

D 187

Number in class: 3

LÜTJENS D185 1969
MÖLDERS D186 1969
ROMMEL D187 1970

Modified Charles F. Adams (Type 103B) Class

Specifications and Technical Data

isplacement, tonnes: 4,720
imensions, metres (feet): 133.2 × 14.3 × 6.1 437 × 47 × 20)
lissiles: SSM: Harpoon missiles for Mk13 SAM uncher
AM: Standard MR SM1 for single Mk 13 launcher aft, tal missiles 40
SW Weapons: 1 × 8 ASROC amidships
uns: 2 × 1 127 mm, one forward, one aft
orpedoes: 2 × 3 324 mm Mk 32 tubes for lk 46 ASW LWT
SW Weapons: depth charge projector aft
onar: DSQS 21 hull-mounted medium-frequency ctive
adar: SPS 40 E/F band air search, SPS 52 3D E/F band r search, SPS 10 G band surface search, SPG 51 G/I and SAM fire control, SPQ 9 and SPG 60 I/J band gun re control
ction Information Organisation: SATIR 1
achinery: 2 × geared steam turbines, 2 × shafts, ,000 hp, 4 × boilers
peed, knots: 32
ange, nautical miles: 4,000 miles at 18 knots
omplement: 337

otograph: *Rommel* 1988 (van Ginderen/Naval Forces)

These three ships of American design were authorised in 1964 and laid down in the United States at Bath Ironworks in 1966 (**D185-6**) and 1967 (**D187**). The ships were launched on 11 August 1967 (**D185**), 13 April 1968 (**D186**) and 1 February 1969 (**D187**). The ships were given major modernisation by H.D.W. and the Naval Dockyard, Kiel, *Mölders* from 1982-84, *Rommel* from 1983-85 and *Lütjens* from 1984-86. This included a new Mk 13 launcher for Standard/Harpoon missiles, digital fire control computers and a higher superstructure abaft the bridge to mount the SPG 60 and SPQ 9 fire control radars. These comprise the Mk 86 gunfire control system which replaced the old Mk 68 installation. The Mk 86 allows a third SAM fire control channel.

Mk 36 6-barrelled chaff launchers were also fitted for electronic countermeasures and an FL-1800S radar intercept ESM. It is planned to fit two RAM advanced point defence missile launchers and the improved DSQS 21B sonar. The ships will remain in service until the early years of the next century.

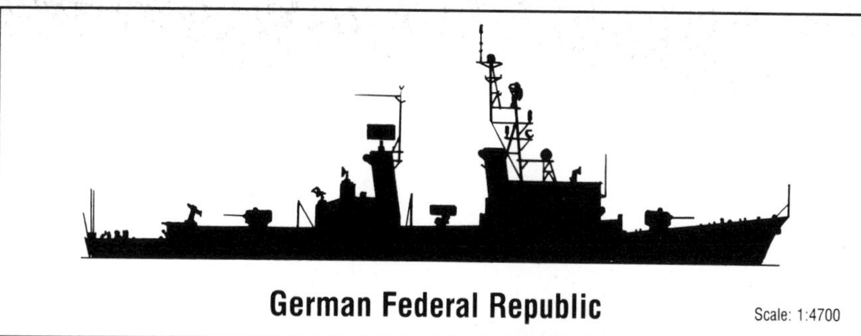

German Federal Republic

Scale: 1:4700

D184

Hamburg (Type 101A) Class

Specifications and Technical Data

Number in class: 4

HAMBURG D181 1964
SCHLESWIG-HOLSTEIN D182 1964
BAYERN D183 1965
HESSEN D184 1968

Displacement, tonnes: 4,750
Dimensions, metres (feet): 133.7 × 13.4 × 6.2 (438.5 × 44 × 20.3)
Missiles: SSM: 2 × 2 MM 38 Exocet aft
Guns: 3 × 1 100 mm 2 forward 1 aft, 4 × 2 40 mm fore and aft amidships
Torpedoes: 4 × 1 533 mm tubes for ASW HWT
ASW Weapons: 2 × 4 375 mm rocket launchers forward, 2 × depth charge projectors and depth charge rails at stern
Sensors: ELAC 1BV hull-mounted medium-frequency active
Radar: LW 04 D band air search, DA 08 F band air/surface search, ZW 01 I/J band surface search, Kelvin Hughes 14/9 I band navigation, M45 I/J band fire control
Machinery: 2 × sets Wahodeg geared steam turbines, 68,000 hp, 2 × shafts, 4 × boilers
Speed, knots: 35 knots
Range, nautical miles: 3,400 miles at 18 knots
Complement: 280

Photograph: *Hessen* 1986 (van Ginderen/Naval Forces)

The primary emphasis of these ships is on anti-surface warfare and short range active sonar ASW. Between 1975 and 1977 the Exocet missiles replaced one of the aft 100 mm gun mounts. Other modifications were a new LW 04 air search radar and light anti-aircraft guns and two extra ASW torpedo tubes. Five fixed anti-ship torpedo tubes in the bows and stern were removed. In the late 1990s they will be replaced by four 4,300 ton Type 123 frigates. The first of the latter was laid down in 1989. The 'Hamburg' class destroyers are fitted for minelaying with stern racks for up to 80 mines. The ships were built by H.C. Stulcken at Hamburg. The first two ships were laid down in 1959 and launched in 1960, the third was laid down in September 1960 and launched in August 1962 and the fourth was laid down in February 1961 and launched in May 1963.

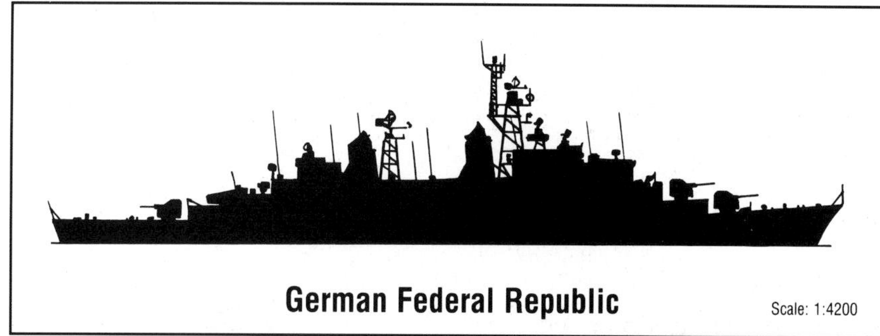

German Federal Republic

Scale: 1:4200

F 212

Specifications and Technical Data

Number in class: 8

BREMEN F207 1982
NIEDERSACHSEN F208 1982
RHEINLAND-PFALZ F209 1983
EMDEN F210 1983
KÖLN F211 1984
KARLSRUHE F212 1984
AUGSBURG F213 1989
LÜBECK F214 1990

Guided Missile Frigates
Bremen (Type 122) Class

Displacement, tonnes: 3.800
Dimensions, metres (feet): 130 × 14.5 × 6.5 (426.4 × 47.6 × 21.3)
Aircraft: 2 × Lynx helicopters
Missiles: SSM: 2 × 4 Harpoon amidships
SAM: 1 × 8 Sea Sparrow forward, 24 missiles, 2 × Stinger multiple launchers
Guns: 1 × 76 mm forward
Torpedoes: 2 × 2 324 mm Mk 32 tubes for Mk 46 ASW LWT
Sonar: DSQS 21 BZ hull-mounted medium-frequency active
Radar: DA 08 F band air/surface search, 3 RM 20 I band navigation, WM 25 I/J band and STIR I/J/K band fire control
Action Information Organisation: SATIR
Machinery: 2 × General Electric-Fiat LM 2500 gas turbines, 51,600 hp, 2 × MTU 20V 956 TB92 diesels, 10,400 hp, 2 × shafts
Speed, knots: 30
Range, nautical miles: 4,000 at 18 knots
Complement: 200

In 1976 it was decided to build the first six of these ships in order to replace the oldest of the surface combatants with which the Bundesmarine had started in the 1950s. The design was based on the Dutch 'Kortenaer' class, although with different machinery. The ships were built at a number of yards, **F207** and **F213** at Bremer Vulkan which fits out the whole class. Basic construction of **F208** was carried out by A.G. Weser, **F209** and **F211** by Blohm & Voss, **F210** and **F214** by Thyssen Nordseewerke, Emden and **F212** by Howaldtswerke, Kiel. Laying down dates were: **F207** July 1979, **F208** November 1979, **F209** September 1979, **F210** June 1980, **F211** June 1980, **F212** March 1981, **F213** April 1987 and **F214** June 1987. Launch dates were, **F207** September 1979, **F208** June 1980, **F209** September 1980, **F210** December 1980, **F211** May 1981, **F212** January 1982, **F213** September 1987 and **F214** October 1987. RAM point defence SAM launchers are to be fitted on the roof of the hangar aft. The Lynx helicopters currently used for torpedo delivery only are to be fitted with DAQS 13D dipping sonar. Sixteen Mk 46 torpedoes are carried for the helicopter and eight for the ship's torpedo tubes. The ships are fitted with American Prairie/Masker systems to reduce radiated noise and they tow the SLQ-25 Nixie torpedo decoy. These are general-purpose units capable of active sonar ASW in shallow continental shelf waters. The Bundesmarine will not acquire towed arrays until the Type 123 frigates enter service in the 1990s.

Photograph: *Karlsruhe* 1986 (van Ginderen/Naval Forces)

German Federal Republic

Scale: 1:4100

F 451

Number in class: 2

ELLI F450 1981
LIMNOS F451 1982

Specifications and Technical Data

Displacement, tonnes: 3,790
Dimensions, metres (feet): 130.5 × 14.6 × 6.2 (428 × 47.9 × 21.3)
Aircraft: 1 × AB 212 ASW helicopter
Missiles: SSM: 2 × 4 Harpoon amidships
SAM: 1 × 8 Aspide, 24 missiles, Redeye shoulder-launched short range
Guns: 2 × 1 76 mm, one forward, one aft (after gun being replaced by Vulcan Phalanx CIWS)
Torpedoes: 2 × 2 324 mm Mk 32 for Mk 46 ASW LWT
Sonar: SQS 505 hull-mounted active
Radar: LW 08 D band air search, ZW 06 I band surface search, WM 25 I/J band and STIR I/J/K band fire control
Action Information Organisation: SEWACO 2
Machinery: 2 × Rolls-Royce Olympus TM 3B gas turbines, 51,600 hp, 2 × Rolls-Royce Tyne RM 1C, 9,800 hp, 2 × shafts
Speed, knots: 30
Range, nautical miles: 4,700 at 16 knots
Complement: 176

It was agreed in 1980-81 to purchase from the Netherlands two of the 'Kortenaer' class 'Standard' frigates under construction for the Royal Netherlands Navy. The two ships chosen were *Pieter Florisz* and *Witte de With*, hulls 6 and 7 of the Dutch programme. The ships had been laid down at the Royal de Schelde Shipyard, Flushing in June 1977 and July 1978, and were launched in December 1979 and October 1979 respectively. *Elli*, formerly *Pieter Florisz*, was taken over by Greece on commencement of her sea trials in June 1981, and entered service with the Greek Navy in October of the same year. *Limnos*, formerly *Witte de With*, was commissioned by the Greeks on 18 September 1982. When the two Dutch-built ships commissioned into the Greek Navy, the main difference was in the hangar area. The hangar itself was extended by just over two metres to accommodate the AB212 helicopter. The Greeks also reverted to a second 76 mm OTO-Melara gun on the hangar roof as in the first two Dutch 'Kortenaers'; this is being replaced by a Vulcan-Phalanx CIWS. The Greeks preferred Italian Aspide missiles to the original Sea Sparrows. Harpoon was not originally fitted. It was decided in 1988 that the West German Meko 200 would be chosen as the future Greek frigate with the first vessel being built by Blom & Voss, Hamburg and the rest in Greece. The first of the 2,800 ton CODOG ships is due for delivery in 1992.

Photograph: *Limnos* (Greek Navy)

210

Number in class: 2

MIAOULIS D211 1971 (1944)
THEMISTOCLES D210 1971 (1944)

Allen M. Sumner and Gearing (FRAM II) Classes

Specifications and Technical Data

Displacement, tonnes: (D211) 3.320 (D210) 3,500
Dimensions, metres (feet): (D211) 114.8 × 12.5 × 5.8 (376.5 × 40.9 × 19); (D210) 119 × 12.6 × 5.8 (390.5 × 41.2 × 19)
Aircraft: 1 × AB 212 ASW helicopter
Missiles: SAM: Redeye shoulder-launched short range
Guns: 3 × 2 127 mm two forward one aft, (D211) 2 × 1 20 mm or (D210) 2 × 2 30 mm, 2 × 1 12.7 mm
Torpedoes: 2 × 3 Mk 32 tubes for Mk 46 ASW LWT
ASW Weapons: 2 × Mk 10 Hedgehog
Sonar: (D211) SQS 29 or (D210) SQS 23 hull-mounted medium-frequency active, SQA 10 medium-frequency variable depth
Radar: SPS 40 E/F band air search, SBS 10 G band surface search, Decca I band navigation, Mk 25 I/J band fire control
Machinery: 2 × geared steam turbines, 60,000 hp, 2 × shafts, 4 × boilers
Speed, knots: 30 knots
Range, nautical miles: 4,600 at 15 knots
Complement: 270

Miaoulis is the former World War II American destroyer USS *Ingraham*. She was laid down at the Federal Shipbuilding and Dry Dock Company on 4 August 1943, launched on 16 January 1944 and commissioned on 10 March that year. *Themistocles* is one of the slightly-enlarged 'Gearing' class destroyers, formerly the USS *Frank Knox*, laid down by Bath Iron Works in May 1944, launched in September 1944 and completed in December 1944. Both received the more austere of the FRAM (Fleet Rehabilitation And Modernisation programme) conversions, and both were sold to the Greeks in 1971, **D211** on 16 July and **D210** on 30 January. The latter had been converted into a radar picket, but this equipment was removed in 1978 and a helicopter hangar added to enhance the ship's ASW potential. The hangar was extended to house the AB 212 in 1987. In 1986-7 *Miaoulis* was modernised to the same standard.

Photograph: *Themistocles* (Greek Navy)
Silhouette: *Miaoulis*

214
ΣΑΧΤΟΥΡΗΣ
214

Gearing (FRAM I) Class

Specifications and Technical Data

Number in class: 6

KANARIS D212 1972 (1945)
KOUNTOURIOTIS D213 1973 (1946)
SACHTOURIS D214 1973 (1946)
TOMPAZIS D215 1977 (1945)
APOSTOLIS D216 1980 (1945)
KRIEZIS D217 1981 (1945)

Displacement, tonnes: 3,500
Dimensions, metres (feet): 119 × 12.6 × 5.8 (390.5 × 41.2 × 19)
Missiles: SSM: (D212-215) 2 × 2 Harpoon aft
SAM: Redeye shoulder-launched short range
ASW Weapons: 1 × 8 ASROC amidships
Guns: 2 × 2 127 mm, one forward, one aft, 1 × 1 76 mm aft, (D216-217) 1 × 1 40 mm forward, 4 × 1 20 mm, 2 × 12.7 mm
Torpedoes: 2 × 3 324 mm Mk 32 for Mk 46 ASW LWT forward
ASW Weapons: 2 × depth charge racks
Sonar: SQS 23 hull-mounted medium-frequency active
Radar: (D212, 215-216) SPS 37 B/C band air search or (D213-214, 217) SPS 40 E/F band air search, SPS 10 G band surface search, Decca I band navigation, Mk 25 and RTN 10X I/J band fire control
Machinery: 2 sets geared steam turbines, 2 × shafts, 60,000 hp, 4 × boilers
Speed, knots: 30 knots
Range, nautical miles: 4,800 at 15 knots
Complement: 269

Former 'Gearing' class destroyers of the US Navy, the definitive American fleet destroyer type of World War II, these ships were given the full FRAM I (Fleet Rehabilitation And Modernisation) conversion in the 1960s into modern ASW escorts. The original names were, **D212** *Stickell*, launched 16 June 1945, **D213** *Rupertus*, launched 21 September 1945, **D214** *Arnold J. Isbell*, launched 6 August 1945, **D215** *Gurke*, launched 15 February 1945, **D216** *Charles P. Cecil*, launched 22 April 1945, **D217** *Miles C. Fox*, launched 13 January 1945. The original builders were Consolidated Steel (**D212**), Bethlehem, Quincy (**D213**), Bethlehem, Staten Island (**D214**), Todd, Seattle (**D215**) and Bath Ironworks (**D216-217**). **D213** and **D214** were not purchased by the Greek Navy until July 1978. The dates above are the dates of transfer. Two similar destroyers were transferred in 1981 to be cannibalised for spares to keep the other ships running. During the 1980s these ships have received major modernisations in which they were fitted with an Oto-Melara quick firing gun aft and a new fire control system. In 1987-8 four of the ships were fitted with Harpoon missiles which necessitated the removal of the forward 40 mm gun which had previously been added.

Photograph: *Sachtouris* (Gyssels Gilbert/USNI)

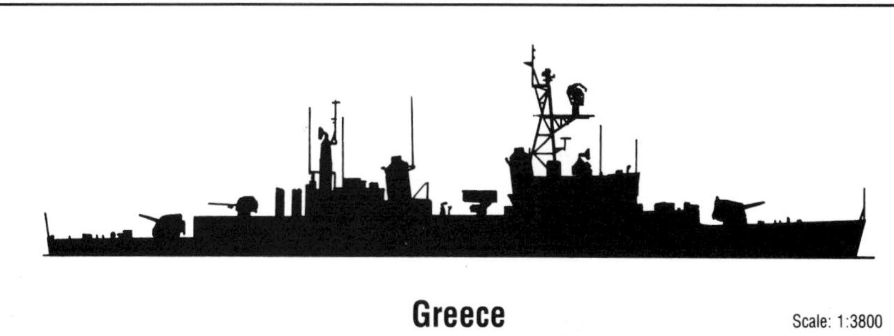

Greece

Scale: 1:3800

06

Number in class: 4

ASPIS D06 1959 (1943)
VELOS D16 1959 (1943)
LONCHI D56 1960 (1943)
SFENDONI D85 1959 (1942)

Fletcher Class

Specifications and Technical Data

Displacement, tonnes: 3,050
Dimensions, metres (feet): 114.7 × 12 × 5.5 (376.5 × 39.5 × 18)
Missiles: SAM: Redeye shoulder-launched short range
Guns: 4 × 1 127 mm, two forward, two aft; 3 × 2 76 mm, one each beam amidships, one aft
Torpedoes: 2 × 3 324 mm for Mk 46 LWT, 1 × 5 533 mm amidships
ASW Weapons: 2 × Mk 10 Hedgehog, 1 × depth charge rack aft
Sonar: SQS 39 or 43 hull-mounted medium-frequency active
Radar: SPS 6 D band air search, SPS 10 G band surface search, Decca I band navigation, Mk 25, Mk 34 and Mk 35 I/J band fire control
Machinery: 2 sets geared steam turbines, 2 × shafts, 60,000 hp, 4 × boilers
Speed, knots: 32 knots
Range, nautical miles: 6,000 at 15 knots
Complement: 250

Photograph: *Aspis* (Greek Navy)

Former World War II American destroyers, **D06**, **D16** and **D56** were launched at Boston Navy Yard in June-July 1942, **D85** was launched by Consolidated Steel, Texas on 2 March 1942. They were taken over by the Greek Navy in 1959-60 but not purchased until 1977. Two other 'Fletchers' were obtained at the same time but these were scrapped in 1981. All are now in reserve and it is doubtful whether any will return to active service as their systems are obsolete. Their main utility would be in gunfire support although their 533 mm torpedo tubes could fire modern NT 37E homing torpedoes. Greece purchased five ex-German 'Fletcher' class destroyers in 1980-81, but all these now been cannibalised for spares. Plans were announced in 1985 to modernise three 'Fletchers' including two of the ex-German ships but these seem now to have been abandoned.

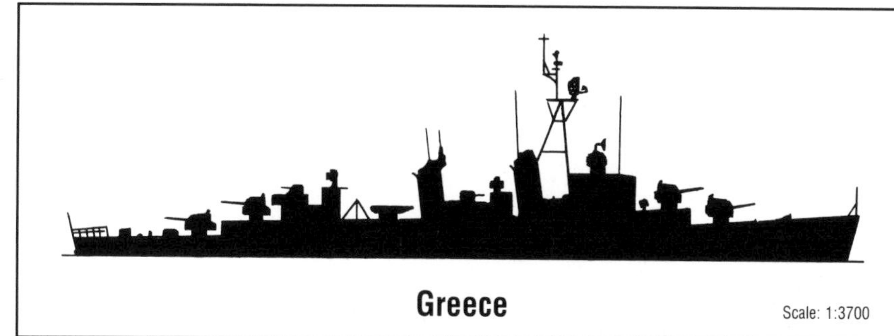

Greece

Scale: 1:3700

01

Number in class: 4

AETOS D01 1951 (1944)
IERAX D31 1951 (1944)
LEON D54 1951 (1943)
PANTHIR D67 1951 (1944)

Specifications and Technical Data

Displacement, tonnes: 1,750
Dimensions, metres (feet): 93.3 × 11.2 × 4.3 (306 × 36.7 × 14)
Missiles: SAM: Redeye shoulder-launched, short range
Guns: 3 × 1 76 mm, two forward, one aft; 2 × 2 40 mm amidships abaft funnel; 7 × 2 20 mm
Torpedoes: 2 × 3 324 mm Mk 32 for Mk 46 ASW LWT
ASW Weapons: 1 × Mk 10 Hedgehog forward, 8 × depth charge projectors, 1 × depth charge rack
Sonar: QCU 2 hull-mounted high-frequency active
Radar: Decca U band navigation, Mk 26 I band fire control
Machinery: 4 × General Motors 16-278A diesels, electric drive, 2 × shafts, 6,000 hp
Speed, knots: 19 knots
Range, nautical miles: 11,500 at 11 knots
Complement: 150

Photograph: *Aetos* (Greek Navy)

Former US World War II 'destroyer escorts', which they were rated at their time of transfer, hence their highly inappropriate destroyer pennant numbers. These obsolete vessels are now only suitable for patrol work and they are first in line for replacement by new construction. They lack modern sensors, but their large number of light guns could lay down a heavy short range barrage that might still be useful in certain Eastern Mediterranean situations. **D01** is the former USS *Slater* and **D31** the former USS *Elbert*. They were laid down at the Tampa Shipbuilding Company on 9 March and 1 April 1943 and were launched on 13 February and 13 May 1944. **D54** and **D67** were built by the Federal Shipbuilding and Dry Dock Company of Port Newark, New Jersey being laid down on 22 February and 23 September 1943, and launched on 25 June and 12 December 1943.

Greece

Scale: 1:3300

03

Frigate
Rhein Class

Number in class: 1 (+ 12)

AEGEON D03 1975 (1962)

Specifications and Technical Data

Displacement, tonnes: 2,740
Dimensions, metres (feet): 98.2 × 11.8 × 4.4 (322.1 × 38.8 × 14.4)
Missiles: SAM: Redeye shoulder-launched short range
Guns: 2 × 1 100 mm, one forward, one aft; 2 × 2 40 mm, one forward, one aft
Torpedoes: 2 × 3 324 mm Mk 32 for Mk 46 ASW LWT
Sonar: Atlas hull-mounted medium-frequency active
Radar: ZW 01 I/J band surface search, DA 01 E/F band target indication, Hughes 14/9 I band navigation, M 45 I/J band fire control
Machinery: 6 × Maybach diesels, 12,600 hp, 2 × shafts
Speed, knots: 20.5 knots
Range, nautical miles: 1,625 at 15 knots
Complement: 110

Photograph: *Aegeon* (Greek Navy)

A former West German combatant tender commissioned into the Greek Navy as an active frigate or 'destroyer escort' hence her 'D' pennant number. She is used as a support ship for fast attack craft for which she can provide logistic and fire support. For self protection she has two 6-barrelled chaff launchers. It is intended that *Aegeon* will be modernised at the Hellenic Shipyard, Skaramanga. This will involve a totally new radar fit and the replacement of the 100 mm guns by 76 mm rapid fire Oto-Melara weapons. She was laid down as the German *Weser* at Elsflether Werft in August 1959 and launched in June 1960. Ten of her sisters remain in service in the Federal Germany Navy as support tenders for missile boats, mine countermeasures ships and submarines.

Two have been transferred to Turkey as a training ship and mine countermeasures support ship. All these other vessels carry 'A' (auxiliary) pennant numbers. These are: German ships – *Lahn* (A55), *Lech* (A56), *Rhein* (A58), *Elbe* (A61), *Main* (A63), *Saar* (A65), *Neckar* (A66), *Mosel* (A67), *Werra* (A68) and *Donau* (A69); Turkish ships – *Sokollu Mehmet Paşa* (former *Isar*) (A577) and *Cezuyinli Gazi Hasan Paşa* (former *Ruhr*) (A579).

Greece

Scale: 1:3100

553

Andrea Doria Class

Number in class: 2

ANDREA DORIA C553 1964
CAIO DUILIO C544 1964

Specifications and Technical Data

)isplacement, tonnes: 7,300
)imensions, metres (feet): 149.3 × 17.2 × 5 489.8 × 56.4 × 16.4)
ircraft: (C553) 4 (C554) 2 × AB 212 ASW helicopters
lissiles: SAM: 1 × 2 Standard SM-1 ER forward
iuns: (C553) 8 × 1 (C554) 6 × 1 76 mm on each beam
orpedoes: 2 × 3 324 mm Mk 32 for Mk 46 ASW LWT
onar: (C553) SQS 23F, (C554) SQS 39 hull-mounted nedium-frequency active
adar: SPS 39 3D E/F band long range air search, RAN L D band air/surface search, RM 20 I band navigation, TN 10X I/J band gun fire control, SPG 55C G/H band nissile fire control
ction Information Organisation: SADOC-1
lachinery: 2 sets geared steam turbines, 2 × shafts, 0,000 hp
peed, knots: 31 knots
ange, nautical miles: 6,000 at 15 knots
omplement: 484

pioneering design of helicopter operating escort ruisers optimised for anti-submarine and anti-air arfare. They were laid down in May 1958, *Andrea Doria* y C.N. Tirreno, Riva Trigoso and *Caio Duilio* by avalmeccanica, Castellammare. *Duilio* was the first to e launched in December 1962 followed by *Doria* in ebruary 1963. During the late 1970s the original Terrier issile system was modernised for Standard extended nge missiles. In 1979-80 *Caio Duilio* was modified to ecome the officers' training cruiser. This involved moving the after pair of 76 mm guns and their associated fire control system and the conversion of the original helicopter hangar into classroom and accommodation spaces. A new hangar was built on the original flight deck, halving the helicopter complement. The ships were not entirely satisfactory in service as their individual aircraft facilities proved too limited for a full cruiser role. Also, despite stabilisers, the small hulls were too lively in heavy seas for all weather helicopter operation. *Caio Duilio* is being replaced by as the training ship by the assault ship *San Giorgio* and is due for early scrapping, but *Andrea Doria* will be retained as the flagship of the Second Division at Taranto until the 'Animoso' class destroyers enter service. She could lead her own task group, but it is nowadays probably better to think of her as a helicopter-capable missile destroyer. In this way she remains a useful addition to one of Italy's pair of Mediterranean 'Gruppi d'Altura'.

Photograph: *Andrea Doria* (S Cioglia/USNI)

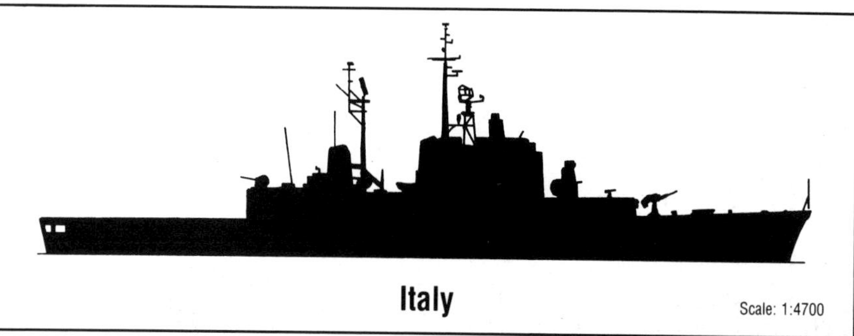

Italy

Scale: 1:4700

Animoso Class

Number in class: 2

ANIMOSO D560 1992
ARDIMENTOSO D561 1993

Specifications and Technical Data

isplacement, tonnes: 5,250
imensions, metres (feet): 147.7 × 15 × 5 (487.4 × 49.5 × 16.5)
ircraft: 2 × AB 212 ASW helicopters
issiles: SSM: 4 × 2 Otomat Mk 2 amidships
AM: 1 × Mk 13 launcher for Standard SM-2, aft 1 × 8 lbatros launcher for Aspide forward
uns: 1 × 1 127 mm forward, 3 × 1 76 mm on each eam and aft
orpedoes: 2 × 3 324 mm ILAS 3 for ASW LWT
onar: DE 1164 integrated medium-frequency active ull-mounted and variable depth
adar: SPS 52C 3D E/F band long range air search, RAN L D band air search, RAN 10S E/F band air/surface earch, SPS 702 I band surface search, RTN 30X and TN 20X I/J band gun fire control, SPG 51D I/J band tandard fire control
ction Information Organisation: SADOC
achinery: 2 × General Electric/Fiat LM2500 gas rbines, 55,000 hp, 2 × GMT BL2300-20DVM diesels, 2,600 hp, 2 × shafts
peed, knots: 31.5
ange, nautical miles: 7,000 at 18 knots
omplement: 400

iese destroyers, originally intended as replacements r the 'Impavido' class, were both laid down at ncantieri at Riva Trigoso on 26 July 1986. Construction s been relatively slow and the *Animoso* was not unched until November 1989. Fitting out is to take ace at Fincantieri's Muggiano yard and the *Animoso* is due to commission in early 1992. *Ardimentoso* is to be launched in 1990. The SM-2 missiles are only the same size as the previous medium range (MR) SM-1 but their range has been tripled to about 75 nautical miles (137 km). This is much better performance than the much larger SM-1 extended range (ER) missiles carried in the larger cruisers. The 76 mm guns will provide an anti-missile capability. Their advanced sonar system will be especially useful in the difficult water conditions of the theatre. Two more ships of the class were projected in 1988 but it now seems unlikely that they will be built. *Animoso* and *Ardimentoso* will now primarily replace the 'Andrea Doria' class cruisers rather than the older 'Impavido' class destroyers, but given the doubts about finding immediate replacements for the latter, they may well act as effective replacements for both classes. The ships' superstructures have been specially shaped to reduce radar cross section and noise reduction measures have also been taken.

Photograph: *Animoso* (Fincantieri)

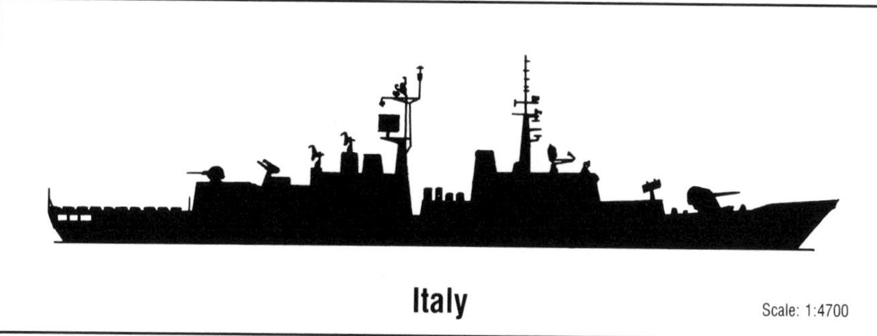

D.550

Number in class: 2

ARDITO D550 1972
AUDACE D551 1972

Specifications and Technical Data

Displacement, tonnes: 4,554 full load
Dimensions, metres (feet): 136.6 × 14.2 × 4.6 (448 × 46.6 × 15.1)
Aircraft: 2 × AB 212 ASW helicopters
Missiles: SSM: 4 × 2 Otomat Mk 2 amidships
SAM: Mk 13 launcher for Standard SM-1 MR aft, 1 × 8 Albatros launcher for Aspide point defence missiles forward
Guns: 1 × 1 127 mm forward; 4 × 1 76 mm, two on each beam
Torpedoes: 2 × 3 Mk 32 for Mk 46 ASW LWT amidships, 4 × 1 533 mm in stern for A184 anti-submarine/anti-surface homing HWT
Sonar: CWE 610 hull-mounted medium-frequency active
Radar: SPS 52C 3D E/F band long-range air search, RAN 3L D band air search, RAN 10S E/F band air/surface search, SPQ 2D I band surface search, SPN 748 I band navigation, RTN 10X I/J band gun and Albatros fire control, SPG 51 Standard fire control
Machinery: 2 sets geared steam turbines, 2 × shafts, 73,000 hp, 4 × boilers
Speed, knots: 33
Range, nautical miles: 4,000 at 25 knots
Complement: 380

Photograph: *Ardito* (S Cioglia/USNI)

Audace was the first of these destroyers to be laid down on 27 April 1968 at the C.N. Tirreno yard at Riva Trigoso. She was launched on 2 October 1971 and commissioned in November 1972. *Ardito* was built by Navalmeccanica, Castellammare being laid down on 19 July 1968 launched on 27 November 1971 and commissioned on 5 December 1972. They are an evolutionary development of the 'Impavido' class and were originally armed with two single Oto-Melara 127 mm (5-inch) guns forward. B mounting was replaced by the Albatros launcher in *Ardito* during a modernisation which was completed in early 1988. *Audace* will complete modernisation to the same standard in 1990. Each Italian 'Gruppo d'Altura' is assigned two or three destroyers and these ships will remain useful additions to the Italian fleet for many years to come. Their good habitability also lends itself to deployment out of the immediate NATO area. For electronic countermeasures the ships carry and integrated jamming and intercept system and an SCLAR 20-barrelled trainable chaff launcher.

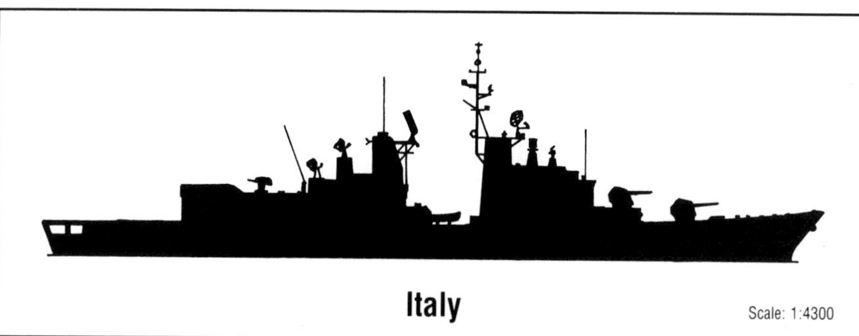

Italy

Scale: 1:4300

D 570

Number in class: 2

IMPAVIDO D570 1963
INTREPIDO D571 1964

Specifications and Technical Data

Displacement, tonnes: 3,851
Dimensions, metres (feet): 131.3 × 13.6 × 4.5 (429.5 × 44.7 × 14.8)
Missiles: SAM: Mk 13 launcher for Standard SM-1 MR aft
Guns: 1 × 2 127 mm forward, 4 × 1 76 mm two on each beam amidships
Torpedoes: 2 × 3 324 mm Mk 32 for Mk 46 ASW LWT
Sonar: SQS 39 hull-mounted medium-frequency active
Radar: SPS 39A 3D E/F band air search, SPS 12 D band air search, SPQ 2A2 I band surface search, SPN 748 I band navigation, RTN 10X I/J band gun fire control, SPG 51 G/I band Standard fire control
Machinery: 2 sets geared steam turbines, 70,000 hp, 2 × shafts
Speed, knots: 33
Range, nautical miles: 3,100 miles at 25 knots
Complement: 335

Photograph: *Impavido* 1986 (L Grazioli/USNI)

Impavido was built under the 1956-7 building programme and was laid down at C.N. Tirreno, Riva Trigoso on 10 June 1957 and launched on 25 May 1962. *Intrepido* was laid down at Ansaldo, Livorno on 16 May 1959 and launched on 21 October 1962. She was built under the 1958-9 building programme. The ships were based on the previous 'Impetuoso' class large destroyers and, like the older pair of ships, they are armed with a rather old-fashioned 38 calibre American 5-inch (127 mm) twin gun mounting. The 'Impavidos' fire control system was modified in the mid-1970s when Standard missiles replaced the original Tartars. Although they are still quite capable as components of Italy's ocean-going task groups they are getting rather old.

It was originally planned to replace them in the early 1990s by the two much more powerful 'Animoso' class destroyers. The latter are now considered more as replacements for the 'Andrea Doria' class cruisers than the 'Impavidos', and the intended replacement for the latter became either a second pair of 'Animosos' projected in 1988, or the first pair of Italian NFR 90 anti-air warfare 'NATO frigates'. Italy withdrew from NFR 90 in 1989 and the extra 'Animosos' seem equally unlikely to be built, therefore these ships may be withdrawn without direct replacement.

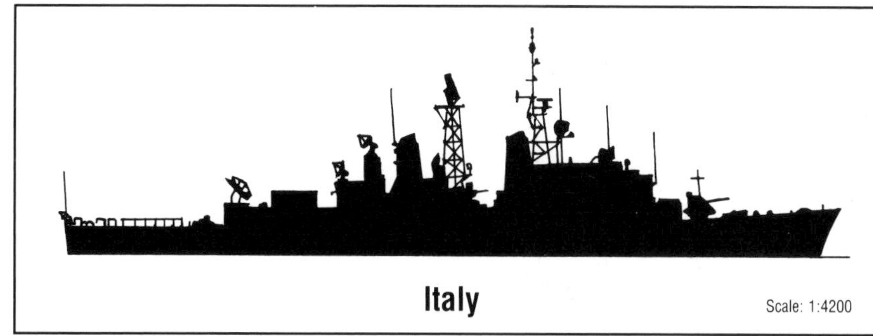

F 577

Maestrale Class

Number in class: 8

MAESTRALE F570 1982
GRECALE F571 1983
LIBECIO F572 1982
SCIROCCO F573 1983
ALISEO F574 1983
EURO F575 1982
ESPERO F576 1984
ZEFIRO F577 1985

Specifications and Technical Data

Displacement, tonnes: 3,040
Dimensions, metres (feet): 122.7 × 12.9 × 8.4 (405 × 42.5 × 27.4)
Aircraft: 2 × AB 212 ASW helicopters
Missiles: SSM: 4 × 1 Otomat Mk 2 aft
SAM: Albatros launcher for Aspide point defence missiles, 24 missiles forward
Guns: 1 × 1 127 mm forward, 2 × 2 40 mm on each beam amidships
Torpedoes: 2 × 3 ILAS 3 tubes for A244 ASW LWT, 2 × 1 533 mm B516 tubes for A184 anti-ship/anti-submarine homing torpedoes
Sonar: DE 1164 medium-frequency hull-mounted and variable depth
Radar: RAN 10S E/F band air/surface search, SPS 702 I band surfce search, SPN 703 I/J band navigation, RTN 30X and RTN 20X fire control
Action Information Organisation: SADOC 2
Machinery: 2 × General Electric/Fiat LM 2500 gas turbines, 50,000 hp, 2 × GMT B 230-20 DV diesels, 11,000 hp, 2 × shafts
Speed, knots: 32
Range, nautical miles: 6,000 at 15 knots, 1,500 at 30 knots
Complement: 230

These ships are enlarged developments of the 'Lupo' class with better hangar facilities and variable depth sonar. This greatly improves their operational capability in the anti-submarine role. All the available armament can be operated efficiently. The slightly slower speed in perfect weather conditions is more than counterbalanced by improved seaworthiness, and higher standards of habitability make for greater crew efficiency. All the ships were built by C.N.R., with all but *Grecale* laid down at the Riva Trigoso yard, and the unfinished hulls being completed after launch at Muggiano. **F571** was laid down at the Muggiano facility. Launching dates for the class were **F570** 2 February 1981, **F571** 12 September 1981, **F572** 7 September 1981, **F573** 17 April 1982, **F574** 29 October 1982, **F575** 25 April 1983, **F576** 19 November 1983 and **F577** 19 May 1984. The DE 1164 hull sonar is a Raytheon produced commercial variant of the US Navy's SQS 56 as used in the 'FFG-7' class combined with VDS operating on the same frequencies as the hull sonar providing an integrated system. The VDS tow cable is 600 metres long and there are plans to extend it by 50 per cent an attach a passive towed array to the transducer. Ships of this class were deployed to the Gulf during the Iran-Iraq War for which duty their armament was increased with two 20 mm guns. The 'Maestrale' class form the backbone of the Italian Navy's 'Gruppi d'Altura' each of which requires five or six frigates. Speed on diesels alone is 21 knots.

Photograph: *Zefiro* (Naval Forces)

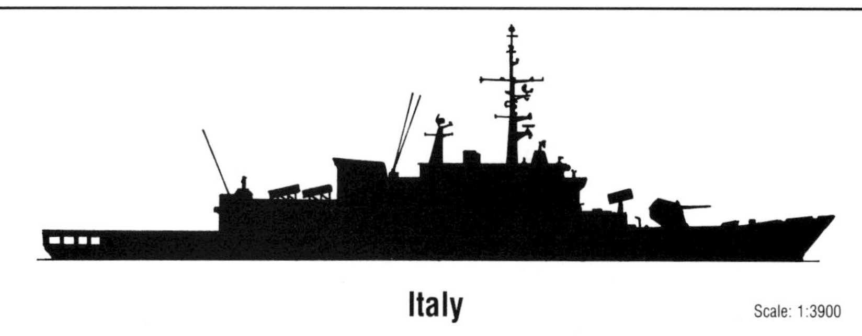

Italy

Scale: 1:3900

F 564

Guided Missile Frigates
Lupo Class

Number in class: 4

LUPO F564 1977
SAGITTARIO F565 1978
PERSEO F566 1980
ORSA F567 1980

Specifications and Technical Data

Displacement, tonnes: 2,525 full load
Dimensions, metres (feet): 113.2 × 11.3 × 3.7 (371.3 × 37.1 × 12.1)
Aircraft: 1 × AB 212 ASW helicopter
Missiles: SSM: 8 × 1 Otomat Mk 2, four on each beam amidships
SAM: 1 × 8 Sea Sparrow aft
Guns: 1 × 1 127 mm forward, 2 × 2 40 mm, one on each beam aft
Torpedoes: 2 × 3 Mk 32 for Mk 46 ASW LWT
Sonar: DE 1160B medium-frequency hull-mounted active
Radar: RAN 10S E/F band air search, SPQ 2F I band surface search, SPN 748 I band navigation, RTN 10X and RN 20X I/J band fire control, Mk 91 Mod I band SAM fire control
Action Information Organisation: SADOC 2
Machinery: 2 × General Electric/Fiat LM 2500 gas turbines, 50,000 hp, 2 × GMT A 230 20M diesels, 7,800 hp, 2 × shafts
Speed, knots: 35
Range, nautical miles: 4,350 at 16 knots, 900 at 35 knots
Complement: 194

Photograph: *Lupo* 1986 (van Ginderen/USNI)

A design of relatively small frigate, based on the previous 'Alpinos', built both for domestic use and export. The 'Lupo' class proved too small for Italy's requirements and was enlarged into the 'Maestrale' design for procurement in the 1980s. The emphasis in capability in the 'Lupos' is on anti-surface warfare hence the heavy missile armament and limited helicopter facilities. Although the ship can in theory operate two helicopters, only one can be fitted in the telescopic hangar and the Italian Navy only allocates a single AB-212 to each ship. The class has sold widely abroad with Peru, Venezuela and Iraq buying a total of fourteen units. The Italian 'Lupos' can fire Aspide missiles from their Sea Sparrow launchers with American fire control systems. Maximum speed on diesels is 21 knots. The first three were built by C.N.R. at Riva Trigoso being launched repectively on 29 July 1976, 22 June 1977 and 12 July 1978. *Orsa* was built at Fincantieri's Muggiano yard being launched on 1 March 1979. The 'Lupos' serve side-by-side with the much-improved 'Maestrales' in Italy's task groups and were deployed to the Gulf in the Iran-Iraq War.

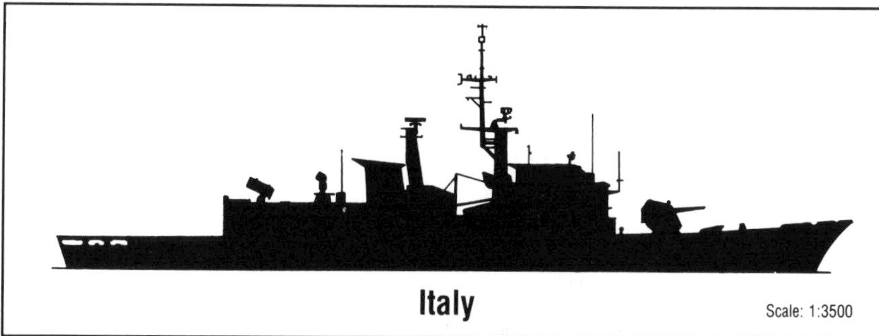

F 581

Number in class: 2

ALPINO F580 1968
CARABINIERE F581 1968

Specifications and Technical Data

Displacement, tonnes: 2,689 full load
Dimensions, metres (feet): 113.3 × 13.3 × 3.9 (371.7 × 43.6 × 12.7)
Aircraft: 1 × AB 212 ASW helicopter
Guns: 6 × 1 76 mm, two forward, four amidships, two on each beam
Torpedoes: 2 × 3 324 mm Mk 32 for Mk 46 ASW LWT
ASW Weapons: 1 × Menon Mk 113 single-barrelled automatic mortar forward
Sonar: DE 1164 integrated medium frequency active hull-mounted and variable depth
Radar: SPS 12 D band air search, SPS 702 I band surface search, SPN 748 I band navigation, RTN 10X I/J band fire control
Machinery: 4 × Tosi OTV-320 diesels, 16,000 hp, 2 × Tosi-Metrovick gas turbines, 15,000 hp, 2 × shafts
Speed, knots: 28
Range, nautical miles: 3,500 at 18 knots
Complement: 244

Photograph: *Carabiniere* (S Cioglia/USNI)

These two ships have been modernised in the 1980s with the latest active sonar and electronic warfare systems. They are thus as capable as the 'Maestrales' in their primary ASW role. Maximum speed on diesels alone is 20 knots. Both ships were built by C.N.T. at the Riva Trigoso yard. **F580** was laid down on 27 February 1963 and launched on 10 June 1967. **F581** was laid down on 9 January 1965 and launched on 30 September 1967. Commissioning dates in 1968 were 14 January and 28 April. Original names for these ships were *Circe* and *Climene*, a reflection of the original intention to build two improved members of the 1950s vintage 'Canopo' class of escort destroyers/frigates. The design was changed several times and eventually resembled an enlarged 'Bergamini' class frigate with gas turbine propulsion to give the higher speed necessary to cope with modern submarines, and larger size to make a better helicopter platform to operate two aircraft. The original helicopters were two AB-204s. A heavy gun armament was also fitted. Originally provided for under the 1959-60 programme two more ships, *Perseo* and *Polluce*, were projected but never built. Italian withdrawal from NFR90 programme now makes a pair of improved 'Maestrales' the likely 'Alpino' replacements.

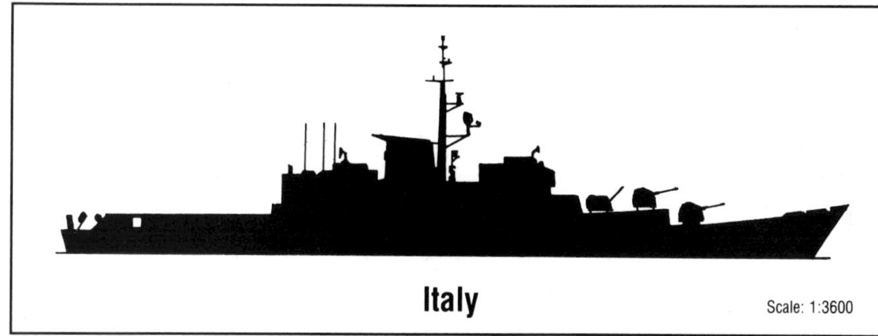

Number in class: 1

VIRGINIO FASAN F594 1962

Frigate
Bergamini Class

Specifications and Technical Data

Displacement, tonnes: 1,650 full load
Dimensions, metres (feet): 95 × 11.4 × 3.2 (311.7 × 37.4 × 10.5)
Aircraft: 1 × AB 212 ASW helicopter
Guns: 2 × 1 76 mm forward
Torpedoes: 2 × 3 324 mm Mk 32 for Mk 46 ASW LWT
ASW Weapons: 1 × Menon Mk 113 single-barrelled automatic mortar
Sonar: SQS 40 hull-mounted medium-frequency active
Radar: SPS 12 G band air search, SPQ 2A2 I band surface search, BX 732 I band navigation and Orion I band fire control
Machinery: 4 × Fiat 3012 diesels, 2 × shafts, 6,000 hp
Speed, knots: 24
Range, nautical miles: 3,000 at 18 knots
Complement: 175

The survivor of a class of four ships, designed to be the smallest hulls capable of helicopter operations. The first three ships, *Carlo Bergamini*, *Carlo Margottini* and *Luigi Rizzo* were laid down in 1957, the first at CRDA, Trieste and the other pair by Navalmeccanica. *Rizzo* was the first to be commissioned at the end of 1961, the other two coming into service the following year. *Virginio Fasan* was the last to be started, being laid down at Navalmeccanica at Castellammare on 6 March 1960 and launched on 9 October of the same year. She entered service on 10 October 1962. She originally mounted three 76 mm guns, but lost the after mount when the telescopic hangar and flight deck were enlarged to take the AB-204 helicopter instead of the smaller AB-47. The AB-212 has since replaced the 204. The 'Bergaminis' were to have been replaced by the 'Maestrales', and *Rizzo* and *Bergamini* were duly scrapped in 1980-81. The other pair were to have followed them by 1983, but were, however, kept in service for the rest of the decade. Only **F594** now remains and she will probably soon be stricken. Originally rated as fast corvettes, these ships were fitted with high-speed diesels rather than the steam turbines of the 1950s vintage 'Canopo' class frigates upon which their hull form was based. The latter's very low freeboard is only suitable for operations in enclosed seas like the Mediterranean

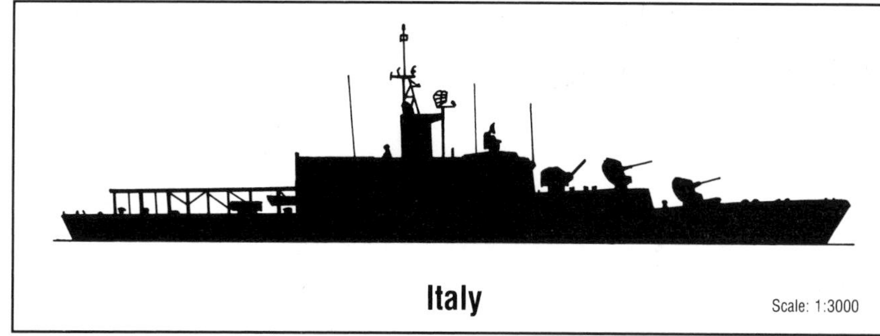

Italy

Scale: 1:3000

Photograph: *Virginio Fasan* 1971 (A Fraccaroli/USNI)

F 551

Number in class: 8

MINERVA F551 1987
URANIA F552 1987
DANAIDE F553 1987
SFINGE F554 1988
DRIADE F555 1990
CHIMERA F556 1990
FENICE F557 1990
SIBILLA F558 1991

Specifications and Technical Data

Displacement, tonnes: 1,285
Dimensions, metres (feet): 86.6 × 10.5 × 3.2 (284.1 × 34.5 × 10.5)
Missiles: SSM: provision for 4 × Otomat launchers amidships
SAM: 1 × 8 Albatros launcher for Aspide missiles aft
Guns: 1 × 1 76 mm forward
Torpedoes: 2 × 3 324 mm B 515 for A244S ASW LWT
Sonar: DE 1167 hull-mounted medium-frequency active
Radar: RAN 10S E/F band air/surface search, SPN 728 I band navigation, RTN 20X I/J band missile fire control
Action Information Organisation: Mini SADOC
Machinery: 2 × GMT BM 2300-20 DVM diesels, 11,000 hp, 2 × shafts
Speed, knots: 24
Range, nautical miles: 3,500 at 18 knots
Complement: 121

Photograph: *Minerva* 1987 (G Valentini/USNI)

The first four of these corvettes were ordered for offshore patrol and training duties in 1982. The first pair was built at Fincantieri yard at Riva Trigoso and the second pair at the same company's Muggiano yard. Dates of laying down were 11 March 1985, 4 April 1985, 26 June 1985 and 2 September 1986. Launch dates were 3 April 1986, 21 June 1986, 18 October 1986 and 16 May 1987. The second group was ordered in January 1987 and three were laid down the following year at the Riva Trigoso and Muggiano yards with the final vessel being laid down Riva Trigoso in 1989. A further four vessels have been planned but it seems likely that they will be replaced by four more of the more austere but helicopter-capable 'Cassiopea' maritime patrol vessels, four of which are currently being built at Muggiano with Merchant Navy funding. There is space in the design for a variable depth sonar to enhance ASW capability. The ships carry a modern ECM suite with an INS-3 jammer/radar receiver and two SCLAR 20 tube chaff launchers.

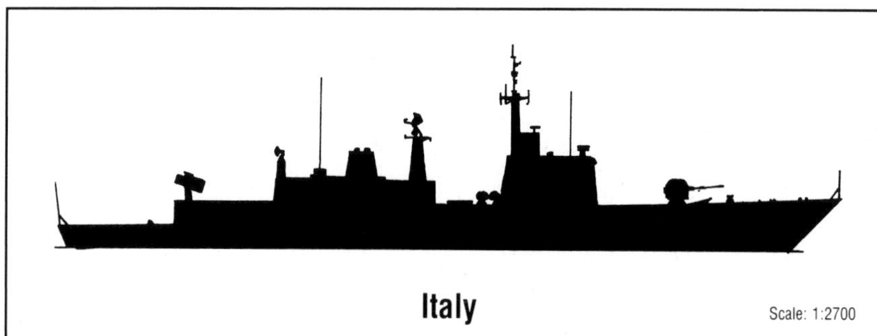

Italy

Scale: 1:2700

F 540

De Cristofaro Class

Specifications and Technical Data

Number in class: 4

PIETRO DE CRISTOFARO F540 1965
UMBERTO GROSSO F541 1966
LICIO VISINTINI F546 1966
SALVATORE TODARO F550 1966

Displacement, tonnes: 1,020 full load
Dimensions, metres (feet): 80.2 × 10.3 × 2.7 (263.2 × 33.7 × 9)
Guns: 2 × 1 76 mm fore and aft
Torpedoes: (except F541) 2 × 3 324 mm Mk 32 for Mk 46 ASW LWT
ASW Weapons: 1 × Menon Mk 113 single barrelled automatic mortar amidships
Sonar: SQS 36 hull-mounted and (except 540) variable depth medium-frequency active
Radar: SPQ 2B I band air/surface search, BX 732 I band navigation, Orion 3 I/J band fire control
Machinery: 2 × (F540-1, 550) Fiat 3012 RSS or (F546) Tosi diesels, 8,400 hp, 2 × shafts
Speed, knots: 23
Range, nautical miles: 4,000 miles at 16 knots
Complement: 129

These ships were enlargements of the older 'Albatros' class. Compared to the earlier design they were built with higher forecastles to improve seakeeping and provide more roomy accommodation for a slightly larger crew. The 'de Cristofaros' were able to mount 76 mm guns without compromising their seaworthiness and they have retained these weapons throughout their lives. They also carried a much improved anti-submarine weapons and sonar fit. The Menon mortar is a 305 mm single-barrelled weapon with automatic loading. It fires 160 kg depth charges out to 900 metres and is especially useful in shallow coastal waters. The double SQS-36 sonar arrangement also was a good fit for conditions in waters close to Italy. Although on the small side for their time the 'de Cristofaros' were effective anti-submarine coastal escorts. They are, however, only corvettes despite their frigate pennant numbers and are of most use today in the coastal patrol role. **F540** was built by C.N. Tirreno at Riva Trigoso, being laid down in April 1963 and launched in May 1965. **F541** was built by Ansaldo at Livorno, as was **F550**. They were both laid down on the same day, 21 October 1962, and were commissioned on 25 April 1966, although **F550** was launched on 24 October 1965, and **F541** on 12 December. The alternative engine fits are both twin high-speed diesels. The ships are faster than the 'Albatros' class, especially in heavier seas. The old 'de Cristofaros' are soon to be replaced by the new 'Minerva' class corvettes.

Photograph: *Pietro de Cristofaro* 1985 (L Grazioli/USNI)

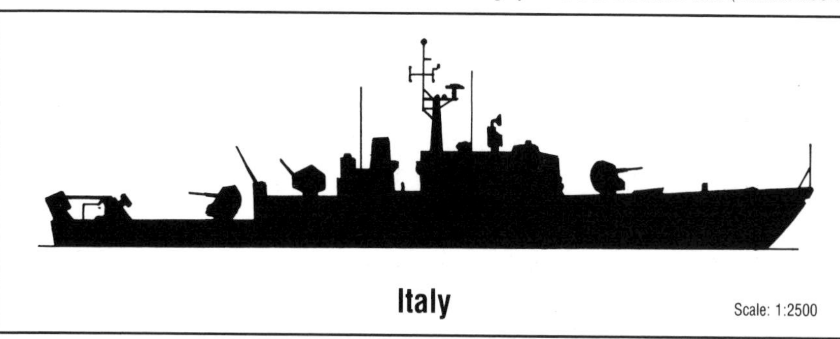

F 545

Albatros Class

Number in class: 3

AQUILA F542 1956
ALCIONE F544 1955
AIRONE F545 1955

Specifications and Technical Data

Displacement, tonnes: 950
Dimensions, metres (feet): 76.3 × 9.6 × 2.8 (250.3 × 31.5 × 9.2)
Guns: 1 × 1 40 mm forward, 1 × 1 and 1 × 2 40 mm aft
Torpedoes: (F542, 545) 2 × 3 Mk 32 for ASW LWT
ASW Weapons: (F542, 545) 2 × Hedgehogs, 2 × depth charge projectors, 1 × depth charge rack.
Sonar: QCU 2 high-frequency hull-mounted active
Radar: SPQ2 I band air/surface search, BX 732 I band navigation
Machinery: 2 × Fiat M 409 diesels, 5,200 hp, 2 × shafts
Speed, knots: 19
Range, nautical miles: 3,000 at 18 knots
Complement: 99

Photograph: *Airone* 1987 (L Grazioli/USNI)

Eight of these coastal escorts were originally built in Italy using American offshore procurement funds in the 1950s. Four were delivered to Denmark, one to the Netherlands and three to Italy. The original armament of two 76 mm guns did not help the seaworthiness of these low freeboard vessels and they were replaced with lighter 40 mm weapons in 1963. The Netherlands, in 1961, had already returned their unit *Lynx* to the calmer waters of the Mediterranean where it became the Italian *Aquila*. One of the Dutch ships, *Diana* was scrapped in 1974, and the other three *Bellona*, *Flora* and *Triton* were replaced by the much more seaworthy and generally more capable corvettes of the 'Nils Juel' class in 1978-81. *Albatros* the Italian name ship of the class was stricken in 1986 and *Alcione* has been converted to a minesweeper, although retaining its 'frigate' pennant number. All four Italian survivors were to have been withdrawn in 1982-83, but the requirement for coastal patrol vessels has led to their retention until they can be replaced by the new 'Minerva' class corvettes and the 1,000 ton 'Cassiopea' class coastal patrol vessels. The latter ships, to carry one 76 mm and two 20 mm guns and an AB-212 helicopter, are being built by Fincantieri to merchant ship standards especially for the constabulary role.

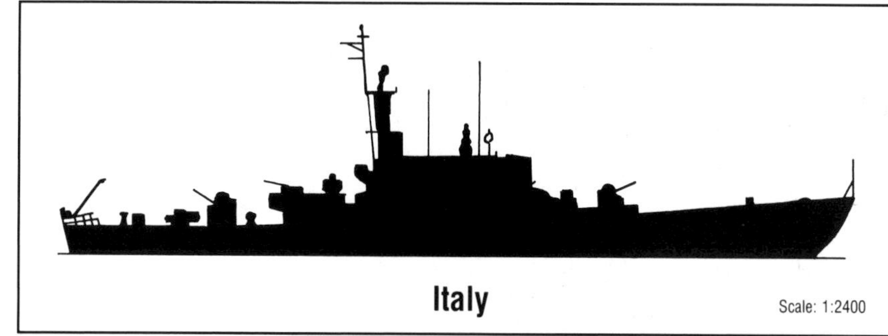
Italy

Scale: 1:2400

F 801

Number in class: 2

TROMP F801 1975
DE RUYTER F806 1976

Tromp Class

Specifications and Technical Data

Displacement, tonnes: 4,308
Dimensions, metres (feet): 138.4 × 14.8 × 4.6 (454 × 48.6 × 15.1)
Aircraft: 1 × Lynx helicopter
Missiles: SSM: 2 × 4 Harpoon amidships
SAM: Mk 13 launcher for Standard SM-1 MR aft, 1 × 8 Sea Sparrow point defence forward
Guns: 1 × 2 120 mm forward
Torpedoes: 2 × 3 324 mm Mk 32 for Mk 46 ASW LWT
Sonar: CWE 610 hull-mounted medium-frequency active, 162M hull-mounted classification
Radar: MTTR/SPS 01 3D F band air/surface search, Decca 1226 I band navigation, SPG 51C G/I band and WM 25 I/J fire control
Action Information Organisation: SEWACO I
Machinery: 2 × Rolls-Royce Olympus TM3B gas turbines, 50,000 hp, 2 × Rolls-Royce Tyne RM1C gas turbines, 8,000 hp
Speed, knots: 30
Range, nautical miles: 5,000 at 18 knots
Complement: 306

Large frigates which are more properly thought of as guided missile destroyers, these ships were built as the flagships for ocean escort groups, providing both command and air defence facilities. The emphasis in the design was on good seakeeping with high freeboard and plenty of volume for electronic equipment and improved habitability. Gas turbine propulsion was chosen over the steam turbines originally planned in order to save personnel. The engine system is similar to that in the contemporary British Type 42s with the Tyne gas turbines used for cruising and the Olympus engines for full speed. The most notable feature of the ships' appearance is the large radome covering the Signaal MTTR/SPS 01 surveillance radar. The ships were laid down in 1971 at the Royal De Schelde Shipyard, Flushing and launched on 2 June 1973 and 9 March 1974. The 120 mm guns are reconditioned mountings from the old destroyer *Gelderland*. The 'Tromps' were to have carried British Sea Dart missiles but the smaller Standard system was chosen instead. The 'Tromps' acquired Harpoon missiles in 1977-8 and in 1984-5 had their electronic warfare suites updated. There were plans to give at least *Tromp* a further modernisation with new radar, but these have been shelved. She will, however, remain in service as the lead ship of one of the three Dutch escort groups. *De Ruyter* is to be placed in reserve in the 1990s.

Photograph: *Tromp* (Dutch Navy)

The Netherlands

Scale: 1:4400

F 812

Specifications and Technical Data

Number in class: 2

JACOB VAN HEEMSKERCK F812 1986
WITTE DE WITH F813 1986

Jacob Van Heemskerck Class

Displacement, tonnes: 3,750 full load
Dimensions, metres (feet): 130.5 × 14.6 × 4.3 (428 × 47.9 × 14.1)
Missiles: SSM: 2 × 4 Harpoon amidships
SAM: 1 × Mk 13 launcher for Standard SM-1 MR aft, 1 × 8 Sea Sparrow point defence forward
Guns: 1 × 1 30 mm Goalkeeper CIWS at stern
Torpedoes: 2 × 2 324 mm Mk 32 for Mk 46 ASW LWT
Sonar: PHS 36 hull-mounted medium frequency active
Radar: LW 08 D band air search, DA 05 E/F band air/surface search, ZW 06 I band surface search, STIR 240 and STIR 180 I/J/K band fire control
Action Information Organisation: SEWACO II
Machinery: 2 × Rolls-Royce Olympus TM3B gas turbines, 50,000 hp, 2 × Rolls-Royce Tyne RM1C gas turbines, 2 × shafts
Speed, knots: 30
Range, nautical miles: 4,700 at 16 knots
Complement: 196

Photograph: *Jacob van Heemskerck* (Dutch Navy)

Given the construction of only two 'Tromps' it was decided to construct an air-defence variant of the 'Kortenaer' class Standard frigate on the thirteenth hull of the class in order to provide a third escort group leader. Plans were changed, however, when the original *Pieter Florisz* and *Witte de With*, hulls 6 and 7 of the 'Kortenaer' class, were turned over to Greece in 1980-1. It was decided to build both replacements as anti-air warfare command ships leaving the thirteenth hull to be added to the 'M' class frigate order. The two ships were allocated the same pennant numbers as those intended for the Greek frigates. Compared to the earlier and larger 'Tromps' these ships lack medium gun armament and aviation facilities. Their Signaal DA 05 radar systems are to be replaced by Signaal SMART 3D sets in 1990. **F812** was laid down at the Royal De Schelde Yard, Flushing on 21 January 1981 and launched on 5 November 1983. **F813** was laid down on 15 December 1981 and launched on 15 August 1984. Commissioning dates in 1986 were 15 January and 17 September respectively. American SQR-19A towed array sonar is to be fitted, although the ships lack organic contact prosecution capacity. These ships will be retained as the escort group flagships in the 1990s with *De Ruyter* going into reserve.

The Netherlands

Scale: 1:4100

F 827

Frigates
Karel Doorman Class

Number in class: 8

KAREL DOORMAN F827 1990
WILLEM VAN DER ZAAN F829 1990
TJERK HIDDES F830 1991
VAN AMSTEL F831 1992
ABRAHAM VAN DER HULST F832 1992
VAN NES F833 1994
VAN GALEN F834 1994
VAN SPEIJK F828 1995

Specifications and Technical Data

)isplacement, tonnes: 3,320 full load
)imensions, metres (feet): 122.3 × 14.4 × 4.3
'401.1 × 47.2 × 14.1)
\ircraft: 1 × Lynx helicopter
Missiles: SSM: 2 × 4 Harpoon amidships
SAM: 16 × Sea Sparrow VLS on port side of hangar
iuns: 1 × 1 76 mm forward, 1 × 1 30 mm Goalkeeper
CIWS on hangar roof, 2 × 1 20 mm
Torpedoes: 2 × 2 324 mm Mk 32 for Mk 46 ASW LWT
Sonar: SQR 18A towed array, PHS 36 hull-mounted
nedium-frequency active,
Radar: Smart 3 ED F band air search, LW 08 D band
ir/surface search, ZW 06 I band surface search, Decca
1226 navigation, STIR I/J band fire control
\ction Information Organisation: SEWACO VII
Machinery: 2 × Rolls-Royce Spey (F827) SM1A (rest)
SM1C gas turbines, 48,000 hp (F827) 37,540 hp,
? × Werkspoor 12 SW280 diesels, 8,000 hp, 2 × shafts
Speed, knots: 29
Range, nautical miles: 5,000 at 18 knots
Complement: 141

Photograph: *Karel Doorman* (Dutch Navy)

These eight ships are intended to replace the older frigates already withdrawn from service by the Royal Netherlands Navy. They will be the towed array units of the Dutch frigate force and will form mixed escort groups with the active sonar 'Kortenaers'. Their construction will bring the Dutch frigate force to its intended total of eighteen units, three groups of six. The contract for construction was signed in June 1985 although the first ship had already been laid down in February at the Royal De Schelde Yard, Flushing. She was launched on 20 April 1988 and is due to commission in the middle of 1990. She will have an interim engine fit and may not have a fully operational action information organisation. They will have accommodation for both male and female crew members plus space for thirty marines. Intended as offshore patrol vessels with their towed arrays they will be capable ASW surface units in the Dutch fleet.

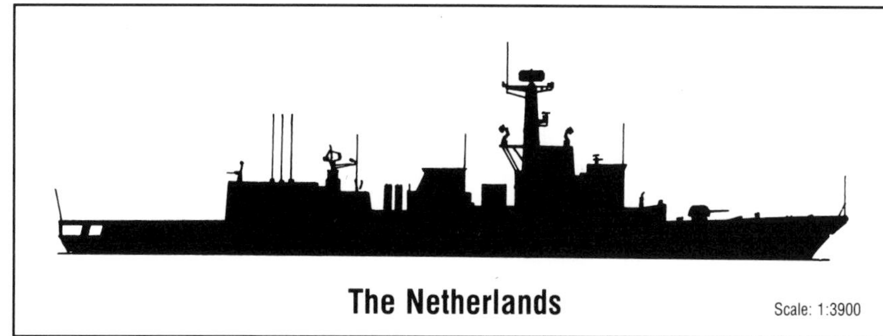

The Netherlands

Scale: 1:3900

F 810

Specifications
and Technical Data

Number in class: 10

KORTENAER F807 1978
CALLENBURGH F808 1979
VAN KINSBERGEN F809 1980
BANCKERT F810 1980
PIET HEYN F811 1981
ABRAHAM CRIJNSSEN F816 1983
PHILIPS VAN ALMONDE F823 1981
BLOYS VAN TRESLONG F824 1982
JAN VAN BRAKEL F825 1983
PIETER FLORISZ F826 1983

isplacement, tonnes: 3,786 full load
imensions, metres (feet): 130.5 × 14.6 × 4.3
428 × 47.9 × 14.1)
ircraft: 2 × Lynx helicopters
lissiles: SSM: 2 × 4 Harpoon amidships
AM: 1 × 8 Sea Sparrow forward
iuns: 1 × 1 76 mm forward, 1 × 1 30 mm Goalkeeper IWS or 1 × 1 40 mm on hangar roof, 2 × 1 20 mm on angar roof
orpedoes: 2 × 2 324 mm Mk 32 for Mk 46 ASW LWT
onar: SQS 505 bow-mounted medium-frequency ctive
adar: LW 08 D band air search, ZW 06 I band surface earch, STIR I/J band and WM 25 I/J band fire control
ction Information Organisation: SEWACO II
achinery: 2 × Rolls-Royce Olympus TM3B gas rbines, 50,000 hp, 2 × Rolls-Royce Tyne RM1C gas rbines, 8,000 hp, 2 × shafts
peed, knots: 30
ange, nautical miles: 4,700 at 16 knots
omplement: 200

wo of these ships will be fitted with towed array to eplace the two towed array 'Van Speijk' ('Leander') ass sold to Indonesia in 1989. Their SQR 18A quipment will be transferred as a temporary fit. Six of e class are to be modernised in 1992-6 and the emaining four will be put into reserve. Normally only ne Lynx helicopter is carried although there is provision r two. The Lynx has a DUAV 4 dipping sonar and is a ery useful ASW detection as well as attack asset. Normally no more than four Harpoons are shipped in peacetime. *Pieter Florisz* was the first of the class to be adapted for female crew. The first two members of the class had a second 76 mm gun mounted on the hangar roof. This was replaced by a Goalkeeper CIWS in *Callenburgh* in 1984 for trials with the system. In the other ships a 40 mm Bofors replaced the heavier gun but this will soon itself be replaced by Goalkeeper in all ships. All but two 'Kortenaers' were built in the Royal De Schelde Shipyard, Flushing. Launch dates for these ships were **F807** 18 December 1976, **F808** 12 March 1977, **F809** 16 April 1977, **F810** 13 July 1978, **F811** 3 June 1978, **F816** and **F825** 16 May 1981, **F826** 8 May 1982. *Philips Van Almonde* and *Bloys Van Treslong* were built in the Wilton-Fijenoord Yard being launched on 11 August 1979 and 15 November 1980. The 'Kortenaers' are general-purpose frigates, though they lack towed array. The ships have a modern ECM capability with Ramses jammers and Corvus and SRBC chaff launchers.

Photograph: *Banckert* (Dutch Navy)

The Netherlands

Scale: 1:4100

F302

Specifications and Technical Data

Number in class: 5

OSLO, F300 1966
BERGEN F301 1967
TRONDHEIM F302 1966
STAVANGER F303 1967
NARVIK F304 1966

Displacement, tonnes: 1,850 full load
Dimensions, metres (feet): 96.6 × 11.2 × 5.5 (317 × 36.8 × 18)
Missiles: SSM: 6 × 1 Penguin at stern
SAM: 1 × 8 Sea Sparrow aft
Guns: 1 × 2 76 mm forward, 1 × 1 40 mm aft, 2 × 1 20 mm in bridge wings
ASW Weapons: Terne III 6 tube trainable automatic mortar forward
Torpedoes: 2 × 3 324 mm Mk 32 for Mk 46 ASW LWT
Sonar: TSM 2633 medium-frequency combined hull variable depth, Terne III high-frequency active attack
Radar: DRRB 22 D band air search, TM 1226 I/J band surface search/navigation, 9LV200 Mk 2 I band tactical fire control, Mk 91 I/J band Sea Sparrow fire control
Action Information Organisation: MSI 3100
Machinery: 1 × set Laval Ljungstrom PN 20 geared steam turbines, 20,000 hp, 1 × shaft, 2 × boilers
Speed, knots: 25
Range, nautical miles: 4,500 at 15 knots
Complement: 150

The class is being modernised to the configuration shown. Dates for completion are **F302** November 1987, **F304** October 1988, **F303** June 1989, **F301** April 1990, **F300** February 1991. The pre-modernisation configuration of these ships was an additional twin 76 mm mounting aft and no VDS. The hull sonar was SQS 36 and the I band tactical and fire control radar was Signaal 22. Chaff launchers are also added at modernisation. The design of these small frigates is based on the American 'Dealey' class destroyer escorts, but with higher freeboard to suit northern sea conditions. Half the cost was met by the United States and the ships were laid down at Marinens Hovedverft between 1963 and 1965. Launch dates were **F300** 17 January 1964, **F301** 23 August 1965, **F302** 4 September 1964, **F303** 4 February 1966 and **F304** 8th January 1965. The Penguin missiles were added during the ships' first major modernisation in the late 1970s. Penguin is a domestically-produced anti-ship missile which uses infra-red homing and has a maximum range in the latest version of 27 kilometres. It is housed in a fibre-glass container-launcher. Terne Mk III is also domestically produced and comprises a special attack sonar, computer and sextuple launcher firing rockets with a range of up to 900 metres. A ripple of six shots is normally fired and reloading takes 40 seconds. These ships are planned for replacement in the late 1990s.

Photograph: *Trondheim* 1988 (van Ginderen/USNI)

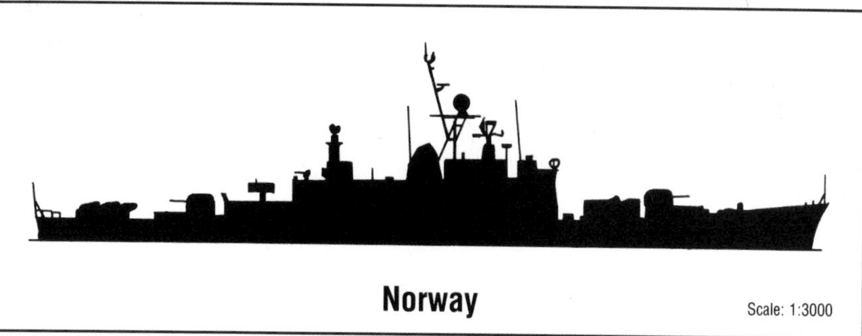

F311

Sleipner Class

Number in class: 2

SLEIPNER F310 1965
AEGER F311 1967

Specifications and Technical Data

Displacement, tonnes: 780 full load
Dimensions, metres (feet): 69.4 × 8.3 × 2.7 (227.5 × 27.2 × 9)
Guns: 1 × 76 mm forward, 1 × 1 40 mm aft
ASW Weapons: 1 × Terne III 6 tube automatic mortar
Torpedoes: 2 × 3 324 mm Mk 32 for Mk 46 ASW LWT
Sonar: TSM 2633 Spherion medium-frequency hull-mounted active, Terne III high-frequency active attack
Radar: TM 1229 I band surface search, Decca 202 I band navigation
Machinery: 4 × Maybach diesels, 8,800 hp, 2 × shafts
Speed, knots: 20
Complement: 63

These are small corvettes which are normally used for training, but in crisis or war both would make useful coastal ASW escorts. The decision to build them was taken in 1959 and they were constructed under the 1960 five-year programme. Five corvettes were originally envisaged, but only two were built. *Sleipner* being laid down in 1963 and *Aeger* (originally named *Balder*) in 1964. *Sleipner* was built by the Nylands Verksted Shipyard, Oslo and was launched on 9 November 1963. *Aeger* was built at the Akers Yard, Oslo and was launched on 24 September 1965. The ships originally carried patrol craft pennants P950 and P951, but received the 'F' numbers subsequent to being fitted in 1972 as specialised submarine chasers. At this time they acquired anti-submarine torpedo armament in addition to Terne. The original American gun fire control system was replaced by two Swedish optronic systems. Originally US AN/SQS sonar was fitted, but this has been replaced in recent modernisation by Thomson-CSF equipment. The refit also included fitting an improved Terne system. *Sleipner* completed her conversion in August 1988 and *Aeger* in May 1989.

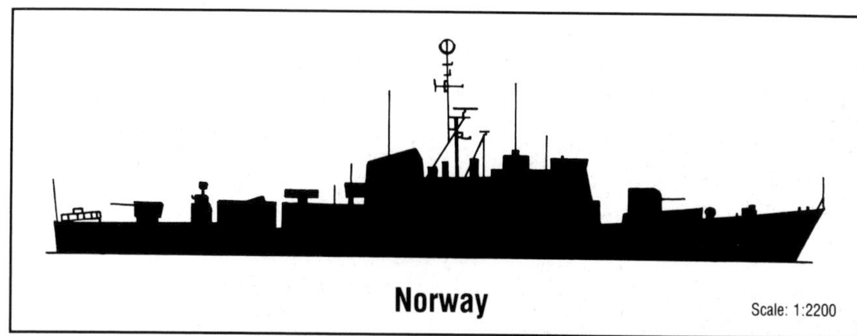

Photograph: *Aeger* 1988 (Gyssels Gilbert/USNI)

Vasco da Gama Class

Number in class: 3

VASCO DA GAMA 1990
ALVARES CABRAL 1991
CORTE REAL 1991

Specifications and Technical Data

Displacement, tonnes: 3,180 full load
Dimensions, metres (feet): 115.9 × 14.8 × 4.1 (380.3 × 48.7 × 13.5)
Aircraft: 2 × Lynx helicopters
Missiles: SSM: 2 × 4 Harpoon abaft bridge
SAM: 1 × 8 Sea Sparrow abaft funnel
Guns: 1 × 1 100 mm forward, 1 × 1 20 mm Vulcan Phalanx CIWS on hangar roof
Torpedoes: 2 × 3 324 mm Mk 32 for Mk 46 ASW LWT
Sonar: SQS 510 hull-mounted medium-frequency active
Radar: DA 08 F band air search, MW 08 F band air/surface search, 1007 I band navigation, STIR I/J/K band fire control
Action Information Organisation: SEWACO/STACOS
Machinery: 2 × General Electric LM 2500 gas turbines, 53,600 hp, 2 × MTU 12V 1163 TB83 diesels, 8,840 hp, twin shafts
Speed, knots: 31
Range, nautical miles: 4,900 at 18 knots
Complement: 184

Photograph: Meko 200 frigate (General Electric/USNI)

These ships, which mark an enormous leap in the capability of the Portuguese surface fleet, have been 60 per cent financed by West Germany, the United States, Canada, Norway and the Netherlands under NATO auspices. The United States is providing the missile, torpedo and CIWS systems. The contract was obtained in July 1986 by a German consortium to build three ships of the Meko 200 type. *Vasco Da Gama* was laid down at Blohm & Voss, Hamburg on 5 August 1988 and the other two ships at Howaldtswerke, Kiel in February and August 1989. The ships will be fully equipped with data links and possibly satellite communications in order for them to play a full part in NATO task forces. The ships have been fitted for towed array sonars and eventual conversion to a vertical launch Sea Sparrow system. The frigates will have a modern ECM suite with intercept and jamming equipment and SRBOC 6-barrelled chaff launchers. There is space in the design for the addition of 25 mm Sea Zenith CIWS forward. These ships are to replace the three US-designed 'Dealey' class frigates built in the 1960s and taken out of service at the end of the 1980s.

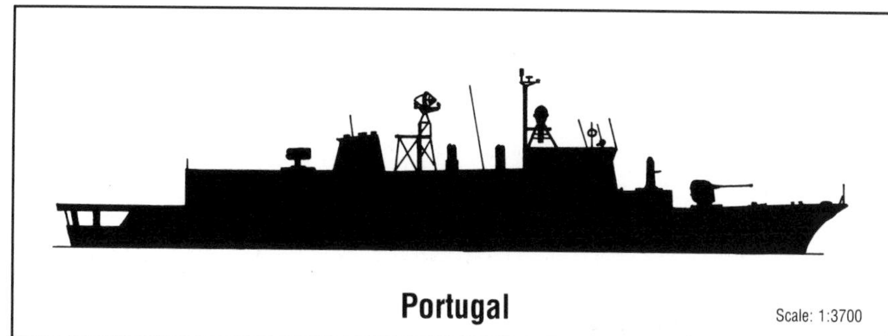

Portugal

Scale: 1:3700

F 480

Comandante João Belo Class

Number in class: 4

COMANDANTE JOÃO BELO F480 1967
COMANDANTE HERMEGILDO CAPELO F481 1968
COMANDANTE ROBERTO IVENS F482 1968
COMANDANTE SACADURA CABRAL F483 1969

Specifications and Technical Data

Displacement, tonnes: 2,250
Dimensions, metres (feet): 102.7 × 11.7 × 4.4 (336.9 × 38.4 × 14.4)
Guns: 3 × 110 mm, one forward, two aft; 2 × 1 40 mm on each side of funnel
ASW Weapons: 1 × 305 mm 4 barrelled automatic mortar forward
Torpedoes: 2 × 3 550 mm for L3 ASW HWT
Sonar: SQS 17A hull-mounted medium-frequency active, DUBA 3A hull-mounted high-frequency active
Radar: DRBV 22A D band air search, DRBV 50 G band surface search, RM 316P I band navigation, DRBC 31D I band fire control
Machinery: 4 × SEMT-Pielstick diesels, 16,000 hp
Speed, knots: 25
Range, nautical miles: 7,500 at 15 knots
Complement: 214

Photograph: *Comandante João Belo* (Portuguese Navy)

Ships of the French 'Commandant Rivière' type built by AC de Bretagne, Nantes — in France private yards build ships for export. The frigates were laid down respectively in September 1965, May 1966, December 1966 and August 1967 and were launched in March 1966, November 1966, August 1967 and March 1968. They were designed as gunboats for Portugal's colonial empire and were fitted for tropical service. The ASW mortar could double as a shore bombardment system. The only major difference between the 'Belos' and the standard French 'Rivières' was the shipping of 40 mm guns amidships instead of the original French 30 mm weapons. In order to improve their capability for Atlantic naval warfare the frigates had their electronics and sensors updated in the late 1980s. Further planned updates including the addition of either a helicopter and hangar, or surface-to-surface missiles have not been carried out. The missiles were to have replaced the after gun armament in two ships of the class; the helicopter and hangar were to have replaced the guns in the other two. The 'Belos' are now getting rather old, but they still retain some utility as active sonar convoy escorts.

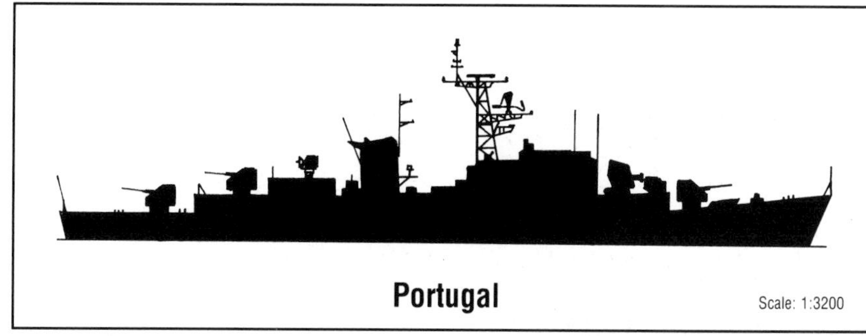

Portugal

Scale: 1:3200

F486

Number in class: 4

BAPTISTA DE ANDRADE F486 1974
JOÃO ROBY F487 1975
AFONSO CERQUEIRA F488 1975
OLIVEIRA E. CARMO F489 1976

Baptista de Andrade Class

Specifications and Technical Data

Displacement, tonnes: 1,348 full load
Dimensions, metres (feet): 84.6 × 10.3 × 3.6 (277.5 × 33.8 × 11.8)
Guns: 1 × 1 100 mm forward, 2 × 1 40 mm aft
Torpedoes: 2 × 3 324 mm Mk 32 for Mk 46 ASW LWT
Sonar: Diodon hull-mounted active
Radar: AWS 2 E/F band air/surface search, RM 316P I band navigation, Pollux I/J band fire control
Machinery: 2 × OEW-Pielstick 12PC2V400 diesels, 10,000 hp, 2 × shafts
Speed, knots: 21
Range, nautical miles: 5,900 miles at 18 knots
Complement: 113

Numbered as frigates, but rated correctly as corvettes, these vessels are modifications of the previous 'João Coutinho' class with improved electronics and weapons. The ships are of the basic Blohm & Voss design intended to patrol off Angola, Mozambique and other parts of Portugal's erstwhile empire. Better equipped than the 'Coutinhos', the 'de Andrades' do retain some ASW capability for use as short-range escorts. Modernisation with surface-to-surface and surface-to-air missiles was planned (the original design had provision for a pair of Exocets) but to date there has only been a communications update. The ships were built in Spain by E.N. Bazan and were laid down in 1972-3, just before Portugal's revolution which was to transform her naval roles. Launch dates were **F486** 13 March 1973, **F487** 3 June 1873, **F488** 6 October 1974 and **F489** 22 February 1974. They were commissioned in November 1974, March 1975, June 1975 and February 1976. After colonial withdrawal was completed, it was planned to sell the 'de Andrades' to Colombia in 1977, where their limited capabilities might have been employed on coastal patrol work, but the deal fell through. There is a flight deck for helicopter operations but no hangar. The Portuguese Air Force operates six C-212 Aviocar helicopters for maritime reconnaissance and maritime duties and these can use the ships as forward operating platforms in favourable weather conditions.

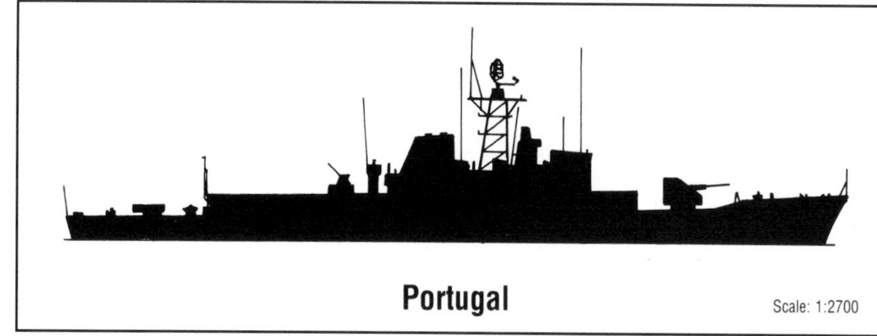

Photograph: *Baptista de Andrade* (Portuguese Navy)

F475

João Coutinho Class

Number in class: 6

ANTONIO ENES F471 1971
JOÃO COUTINHO F475 1970
JACINTO CANDIDO F476 1970
GENERAL PEREIRA D'ECA F477 1970
AUGUSTO CASTILHO F484 1970
HONORIO BARRETO F485 1971

Specifications and Technical Data

Displacement, tonnes: 1,401
Dimensions, metres (feet): 84.6 × 10.3 × 3.6 (277.5 × 33.8 × 11.8)
Guns: 1 × 2 76 mm forward, 1 × 2 40 mm aft
Radar: MLA 1B air search, RM 1226C I band surface search, SPG 34 I/J band fire control
Machinery: 2 × OEW-Pielstick 12PC2V280 diesels. 10,560 hp, 2 × shafts
Speed, knots: 24
Range, nautical miles: 5,900 miles at 18 knots
Complement: 92

Numbered as frigates but rated as corvettes, these ships were built as gunboats to patrol off the colonies carrying a detachment of 34 marines. They replaced Portugal's pre-war sloops and gunboats. What limited ASW potential they had, a QC U2 sonar, Hedgehog and depth charge racks, has been removed and the vessels are now solely patrol ships. Plans to modernise with surface-to-surface missiles and point defence SAMs have been shelved although electronics and communications are being updated. A helicopter can be operated from a flight deck aft and a small landing party of thirty marines can be carried if required. Three of these ships were built by E.N. Bazan in Spain, **F471** launched in August 1969, **F484** launched in July 1969 and **F485** launched in April 1970. The other three were built by Blohm & Voss at Hamburg in West Germany. **F475** was launched in May 1969, **F476** in June 1969 and **F477** in July 1969.
A platform is fitted to allow the operation of a land-based Aviocar helicopter. It was originally intended to operate the larger more manpower-intensive 1960s vintage 'Dealey' type frigates of the 'Almirante Pereira da Silva' class in the offshore surveillance and rescue role but the 'Coutinho' class frigates provide a more cost-effective means of fulfilling this mission. The larger frigates have thus been withdrawn.

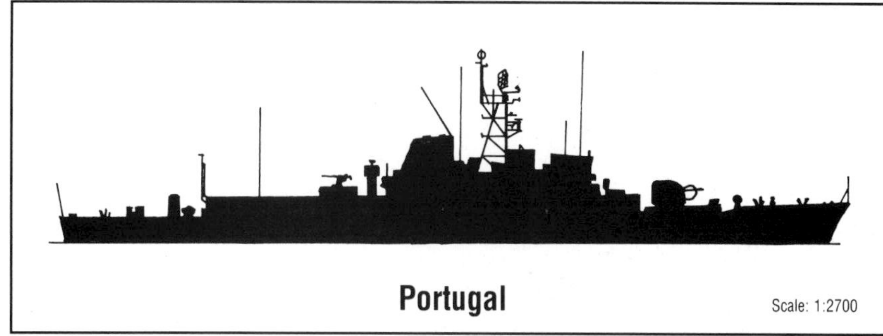

Photograph: *João Coutinho* (Portuguese Navy)

F81

Santa Maria Class

Specifications and Technical Data

Number in class: 4

SANTA MARIA F81 1986
VICTORIA F82 1987
NUMANCIA F83 1988
REINA SOFIA F84 1991

Displacement, tonnes: 4,017 full load
Dimensions, metres (feet): 137.7 × 14.0 × 7.5 (451.2 × 46.9 × 24.6)
Aircraft: 2 × S-70L Sea Hawks
Missiles: SSM: 8 × Harpoon carried in magazine for Mk 13 launcher
SAM: 1 × Mk 13 launcher forward for Standard SM-1 MR, 32 missiles
Guns: 1 × 1 76 mm amidships, 1 × 1 20 mm 12-barrelled Meroka CIWS system on hangar roof
Torpedoes: 2 × 3 324 mm Mk 32 for Mk 46 ASW LWT
Sonar: SQR 19 towed array, DE 1160B hull-mounted medium-frequency active
Radar: SPS 49 C/D band air search, SPS 64V I band surface search, Raytheon I/J band navigation, Mk 92 Mod 2 and STIR I/J band fire control, RAN 12L and VPS 2 Meroka fire control
Action Information Organisation: IPN 10
Machinery: 2 × General Electric LM 2500 gas turbines, 40,000 hp, 1 × shaft, 1 × 800 hp auxiliary motor with retractable propeller
Speed, knots: 29 knots
Range, nautical miles: 4,500 miles at 20 knots
Complement: 223

Photograph: *Santa Maria* (Spanish Navy)

These ships are Spanish-built versions of the American FFG 7 'Oliver Hazard Perry' class. Three were ordered from Bazan, Ferrol in 1977 but the programme was delayed because of the construction of the carrier *Principe de Asturias*. The first ship was not laid down until 23 May 1982 and launched on 24 November 1984. The second was laid down on 16 August 1983 and launched on 23 July 1986. The third frigate was not, however, laid down until 8 January 1986, although it was launched only just over a year later on 30 January 1987. The fourth unit, ordered in the middle of 1986, was laid down on 9 August 1987 and launched in 1989. These four vessels are up to the standards of the later ships in the FFG 7 series having the length and hull of these ships. The main differences are the Spanish CIWS, modified radar and electronic warfare systems (the latter consists of a Nettunel ESM/ECM and four SRBOC 6-barrelled chaff launchers). Satellite communications are not fitted although data link equipment (Link 11) is, which allows integrated operations with the carrier. The sonar is the Raytheon export variant of SQS 56 with some Spanish parts. Spain is ordering two additional ships of this class, F85 and F86, to be fitted with new Spanish action information systems.

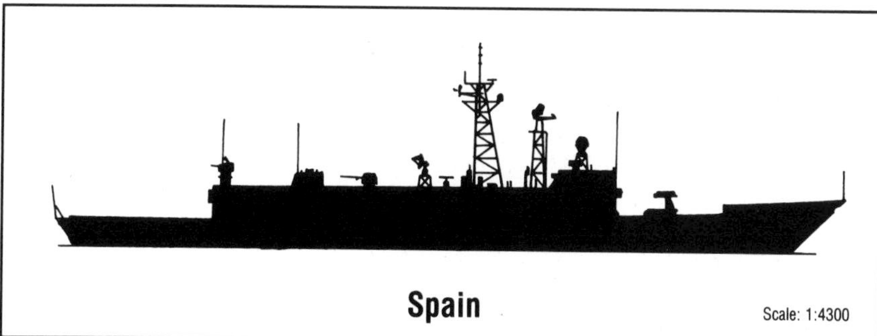

F74

Number in class: 5

BALEARES F71 1973
ANDALUCIA F72 1974
CATALUÑA F73 1975
ASTURIAS F74 1975
EXTREMADURA F75 1976

Specifications and Technical Data

Displacement, tonnes: 4,177 full load
Dimensions, metres (feet): 133.6 × 14.3 × 4.7 (438 × 46.9 × 15.4)
Missiles: SSM: (F71) 2 × 4 (rest) 1 × 4 Harpoon
SAM: Mk 22 launcher for Standard SM-1 MR, 16 missiles
ASW Weapons: 1 × 8 ASROC forward, 8 reloads
Guns: 1 × 1 127 mm forward, 2 × 12-barrelled Meroka 20 mm CIWS one each beam
Torpedoes: 2 × 2 324 mm Mk 32 for Mk 46 ASW LWT, 1 × 2 484 mm Mk 25 at stern for Mk 37 ASW, 41 torpedoes carried of both types
Sonar: DE 1164 integrated medium-frequency active hull-mounted and variable depth, SQS 35V medium-frequency active variable depth
Radar: SPS 52A 3D E/F band air search, SPS 10 G band surface search, Pathfinder I/J band navigation, SPG 53B I/J band and SPG 51C G/I band fire control, RAN 12L and VPS 2 Meroka fire control
Action Information Organisation: Tritan 1
Machinery: 1 set Westinghouse geared steam turbines, 1 × shaft, 35,000 hp, 2 × boilers
Speed, knots: 28
Range, nautical miles: 4,500 at 20 knots
Complement: 256

hese ships are guided missile versions of the American Knox' class frigates and were built with American aid ollowing an agreement of 1966. They substituted a artar surface-to-air missile system, later updated with tandard SM-1 missiles, for the helicopter facilities of the American ships. They are thus less capable anti-submarine platforms than the normal FF 1052s.

The 'Baleares' class is being modernised with new sonar (the original sonars were SQS 23 and SQS 35). SRBOC chaff launchers, improved ESM and ECM systems, modified AIO, Meroka CIWS for point air defence and Link 11. The first to be completed was *Asturias* in 1988. The completion dates for the other members of the class are: *Extremadura* July 1989, *Cataluña* December 1989, *Baleares* July 1990 and *Andalucia* February 1991. The Table refers to the modernised ships which are useful members of 'Grupo Aeronavale Alfa'. All five guided missile frigates were built at the Bazan Yard at Ferrol, being laid down in October 1968 (**F71**), July 1969 (**F72**), August 1970 (**F73**), March 1971 (**F74**) and November 1971 (**F75**). Launch dates were 20 August 1970 (**F71**), 30 March 1971 (**F72**), 3 November 1971 (**F73**), 13 May 1972 (**F74**) and 21 November 1972 (**F75**). Hulls and machinery were built in Spain, but the weapons and sensors came from America.

Photograph: *Asturias* 1987 (van Ginderen/USNI)

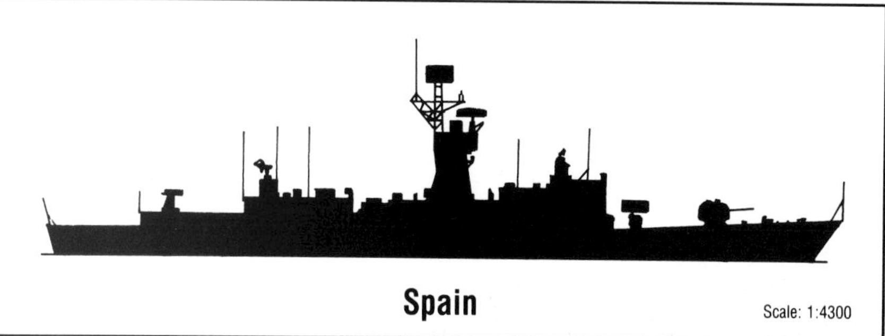

Spain

Scale: 1:4300

F35
F35

Descubierta Class

Specifications and Technical Data

Number in class: 6

DESCUBIERTA F31 1978
DIANA F32 1979
INFANTA ELENA F33 1980
INFANTA CRISTINA F34 1980
CAZADORA F35 1981
VENCEDORA F36 1982

Displacement, tonnes: 1,575 full load
Dimensions, metres (feet): 88.8 × 10.4 × 3.8 (291.3 × 34 × 12.5)
Missiles: SSM: 2 × 4 Harpoon amidships
SAM: 1 × 8 Albatros for 24 Sea Sparrow
Guns: 1 × 1 76 mm forward, 1 × 1 40 mm aft, 1 × 1 Meroka 12-barrelled 20 mm CIWS or 40 mm aft
Torpedoes: 2 × 3 324 mm Mk 32 for Mk 46 ASW LWT
ASW Weapons: 1 × 375 mm twin-barrelled rocket launcher
Sonar: DE 1160B hull-mounted medium-frequency active
Radar: DA 05/2 E/F band air/surface search, ZW 06 I band navigation, WM 22/41 or WM 25 I/J band fire control, RAN 12L I band and VPS 2 Meroka fire control if weapon fitted
Action Information Organisation: SEWACO
Machinery: 4 × MTU-Bazan 16MA956 TB91 diesels, 16,000 hp, 2 × shafts
Speed, knots: 25
Range, nautical miles: 4,000 at 18 knots
Complement: 116

Photograph: *Cazadora* (S Cioglia/USNI)

These ships are based upon the Portuguese 'João Coutinho' class of colonial gunboats. The design has, however, been enlarged to increase its combat-worthiness and the ships are capable of operating in the battle group. They are more suitable, however, for coastal escort operations. Much work has been done to silence them, to improve the performance of their sonar and to make them less vulnerable to enemy acoustic detection. Two of the original order were sold to Egypt prior to completion, and one was ordered and purchased by Morocco. The class is a well-armed surface combatant. The first four were built by Bazan, Cartagena and the last two by Bazan, Ferrol. Launch dates were **F31** July 1975, **F32** January 1976, **F33** September 1976, **F34** April 1977, **F35** October 1978 and **F36** April 1979. A larger 2,150 ton, gas turbine powered, helicopter-equipped development has been seriously considered. When modernised the Meroka CIWS replaced the 40 mm gun mounted aft of the mainmast. **F34** was the first to be so equipped.

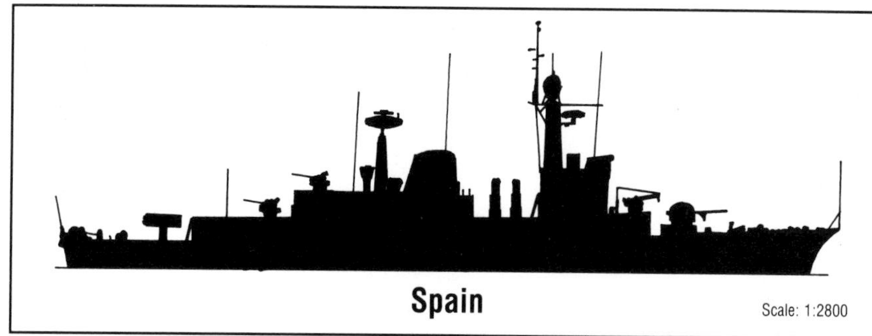

D64

Gearing (FRAM I) Class

Specifications and Technical Data

Number in class: 5

CHURRUCA D61 1972 (1945)
GRAVINA D62 1972 (1945)
MENDEZ NUÑEZ D63 1973 (1945)
LANGARA D64 1973 (1945)
BLAS DE LEZO D65 1973 (1945)

Displacement, tonnes: 3,520 full load
Dimensions, metres (feet): 119 × 12.4 × 5.8 (390.5 × 40.9 × 5.8)
Aircraft: 1 × Hughes 500M helicopter
Missiles: ASW Weapons: (except D65) 1 × 8 ASROC amdships
Guns: 2 or 3 (D65) × 2 127 mm
Torpedoes: 2 × 3 324 mm Mk 32 for Mk 46 ASW LWT
Sonar: SQS 23 hull-mounted medium-frequency active
Radar: SPS 37 B/C band or (D61-2) SPS 40 E/F band air search, SPS 10 G band surface search, Mk 25 or Mk 28 I/J band fire control
Machinery: 2 × sets geared steam turbines, 60,000 hp, 2 × shafts, 4 × boilers
Speed, knots: 31
Range, nautical miles: 4,800 at 15 knots
Complement: 274

Photograph: *Langara* (Spanish Navy)

These old American destroyers were originally transferred on loan, but were purchased in May 1978. They have some limited ASW potential but are really more suitable for patrol and presence duties. *Blas de Lezo*, with its heavier gun armament and no ASROC is normally employed on constabulary duties in Spain's Exclusive Economic Zone (EEZ). She carries her helicopter for surveillance duties, but the others have normally ceased to do so. Their withdrawal from service is imminent. The original names of the ships were, **D61** *Eugene A. Greene*, **D62** *Furse*, **D63** *O'Hare*, **D64** *Leary* and **D65** *Noa*. Launch dates were 18 March 1945 (Federal Shipbuilding, Newark), 9 March 1945, 22 June 1945, 20 January 1945 (all Consolidated Steel, Orange, Texas) and 30 July 1945 (Bath Ironworks). The Spanish-built and designed destroyer, *Marques de la Ensenada*, laid down in 1951, launched in 1959, relaunched after reconstruction in 1968 and finally recommissioned in 1970, is of similar capability to the 'Gearings', was originally scheduled to serve into the 1990s.

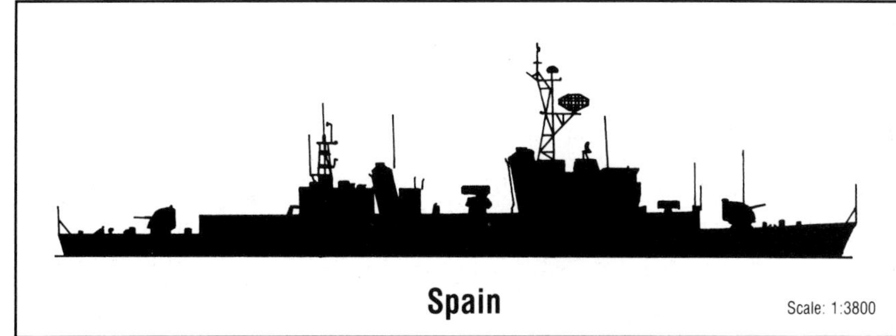

Spain

Scale: 1:3800

F240
F240

Yavuz Class

Number in class: 4

YAVUZ F240 1987
TURGUT REIS F241 1988
FATIH F242 1988
YILDIRIM F243 1989

Specifications and Technical Data

Displacement, tonnes: 2,784 full load
Dimensions, metres (feet): 110.5 × 14.2 × 4.1 (362.4 × 46.6 × 13.5)
Aircraft: 1 × AB 212 ASW helicopter
Missiles: SSM: 2 × 4 Harpoon amidships
SAM: 1 × 8 Sea Sparrow aft, 24 Aspide missiles
Guns: 1 × 1 127 mm forward, 3 × quadruple 25 mm Sea Zenith CIWS, one forward, two aft
Torpedoes: 2 × 3 324 mm Mk32 for Mk 46 ASW LWT
Sonar: DE 1160B hull-mounted medium-frequency active
Radar: DA 08 F band air search, AW 6 G band air/surface search, STIR I/J/K band and WM 25 I/J band fire control, Seaguard I/J band CIWS
Action Information Organisation: SEWACO
Machinery: 4 × MTU 20V 1163 TV93 diesels, 40,000 hp, 2 × shafts
Speed, knots: 27
Range, nautical miles: 4,100 at 18 knots
Complement: 180

Photograph: *Yavuz* 1987 (H Ehlers/USNI)

These are the most capable surface combatants in the Turkish Navy having been ordered at the end of 1982 from a German consortium, Blohm & Voss, Howaldtswerke and Thyssen, Rheinstahl. The first unit was laid down at Blohm & Voss on 30 May 1985 and launched on 7 November that year. The second was laid down at Howaldtswerke on 20 May 1985 and was launched on 30 May 1986. The second pair of ships have been built in Turkey with German technical assistance at the Golcuk Yard. **F242** was laid down on 1 January 1986 and launched on 24 April 1987 and **F243** was laid down on 24 April 1987 and launched on 22 July 1988. The Turks plan to replace their surface fleet with this design and two more were ordered from Golcuk at the beginning of 1989. Up to six additional ships are projected. The design is the Meko 200 as sold by the same consortium to Portugal and Greece. The AB 212 helicopters can double in the anti-surface ship role with Sea Skua missiles. The sonar is the Raytheon export variant of the SQS 56 used in the American FFG 7 frigates.

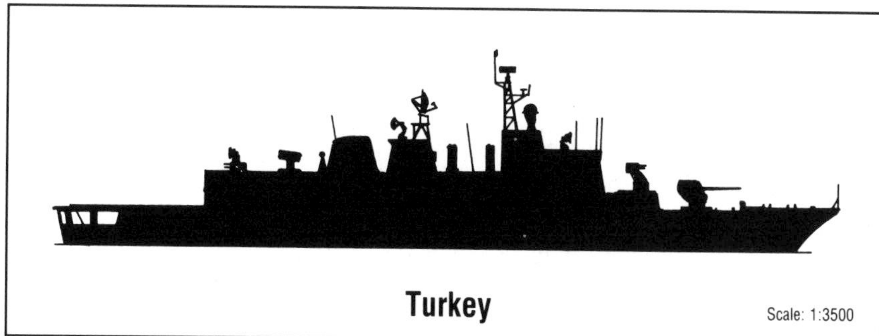

D347
D347

Carpenter (FRAM I) Class

Number in class: 2

ALCITEPE D346 1982 (1949)
ANITEPE D347 1981 (1949)

Specifications and Technical Data

Displacement, tonnes: 3,540 full load
Dimensions, metres (feet): 119 × 12.5 × 6.4 (390.5 × 41 × 20.5)
Aircraft: 1 × AB 212 ASW helicopter
Missiles: ASW Weapons: 1 × 8 ASROC amidships
Guns: 1 × 2 127 mm forward, 1 × 2 76 mm aft, 1 × 2 35 mm forward
Torpedoes: 2 × 3 324 mm Mk32 for Mk 46 ASW LWT
ASW Weapons: 1 × 9 charge depth charge rack at stern
Sonar: SQS 23 hull-mounted medium-frequency active
Radar: SPS 40 E/F band air search, SPS 10 G band surface search, Mk 35 I/J band fire control
Machinery: 2 × General Electric geared steam turbines, 60,000 hp, 2 × shafts, 4 × boilers
Speed, knots: 34
Range, nautical miles: 5,800 at 12 knots
Complement: 275

Photograph: *Anitepe* 1982 (van Gilderen/USNI)

These two ships, laid down as 'Gearing' class vessels in 1945, were completed at the end of 1949 as prototype anti-submarine hunter-killer destroyers (DDK, reclassified DDE in 1950). They were given a totally different armament of 76 mm guns and ASW weapons. Their original names were *Carpenter* (**D347**) and *Robert A. Owens* (**D346**). Both received FRAM I conversions in the early 1960s which made them more like their standard 'Gearing' sisters. The dates above are those of transfer to the Turkish Navy. Both ships were not finally purchased until 1988. Both have received modifications in Turkey such as the Oerlikon 35 mm mounting in B position. The two 'Carpenters', unlike the other 'Gearing' type ships in the Turkish Navy, have large hangars and operate helicopters. This is a significant enhancement to their ASW potential. These ships may be modernised with Sea Sparrow point defence SAMs. **D346** was laid down at Bath Ironworks on 29 October 1945 and launched on 15 July 1946, **D347** was laid down by Consolidated Steel, Orange, Texas on 30 July 1945 and launched on 20 December 1945.

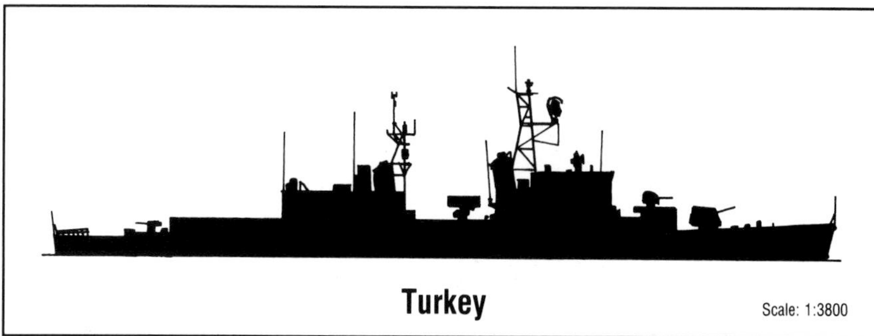

D345

Gearing (FRAM I) Class

Specifications and Technical Data

Number in class: 7

YUCETEPE D345 1983 (1945)
SAVASTEPE D348 1981 (1945)
KILIÇ ALI PAŞA D349 1981 (1946)
PIYALE PAŞA D350 1981 (1945)
M. FEVZI ÇAKMAK D351 1973 (1946)
GAYRET D352 1973 (1946)
ADATEPE D353 1971 (1946)

Displacement, tonnes: 3,600 full load
Dimensions, metres (feet): 119 × 12.6 × 5.8 (390.5 × 41.2 × 19)
Missiles: SSM: (D351-2) 2 × 4 Harpoon aft
ASW Weapons: 1 × 8 ASROC amidships
Guns: 2 × 2 127 mm, one forward, one aft (except D348 both forward), (D353) 1 × 2 40 mm forward, (D351-2) 2 × 2 35 mm fore and aft, remainder 1 × 2 35 mm aft (except D345 forward)
Torpedoes: 2 × 3 324 mm Mk32 for Mk 46 ASW LWT
ASW Weapons: 1 × 9 charge depth charge rack at stern
Sonar: SQS 23 hull-mounted medium-frequency active
Radar: SPS 40 E/F band air search, SPS 10 G band surface search, I band navigation, Mk 25 I/J band fire control
Machinery: 2 × sets geared steam turbines, 2 × shafts, 60,000 hp, 4 × boilers
Speed, knots: 32
Range, nautical miles: 4,800 at 15 knots
Complement: 274

These ships are 'Gearing' class destroyers of wartime design given the more extensive FRAM I conversion in the early 1960s. The first batch was delivered in the early 1970s, purchased in 1973 and modified by the Turks with 40 mm light guns forward and 35 mm weapons aft. Two of these ships have since been further modified with Harpoon missiles, which has necessitated the replacement of the forward Bofors mount by a second 35 mm system. *Sevastepe* was purchased for cannibalisation in 1980 but it was decided to commission her for service the following year. She has the Mk 38 turrets forward and was fitted with a 35 mm mounting in Y position. Another ship was purchased for spares in 1982. **D349** and **D350** were leased for five years in June 1980 and entered service in July of the following year. **D345** was leased in 1982 and commissioned in 1983. They were not given extensive modifications, but had one twin 35 mm mounting added aft. **D345-349** were built by Consolidated Steel, Orange, Texas. Launch dates were May 1945, June 1945 and November 1945. **D350** was built by Bath Ironworks being launched on 8 September 1945. **D351** was built by Bethlehem Steel, Quincy and launched on 15 May 1945. **D352** was built by Todd, Seattle and was launched on 8 January 1946. **D353** was built by Bethlehem Steel, Staten Island and launched on 17 January 1946.

Photograph: *Yucetepe* 1987 (L Grazioli/USNI)
Silhouette: *Çakmak* and *Gayret*

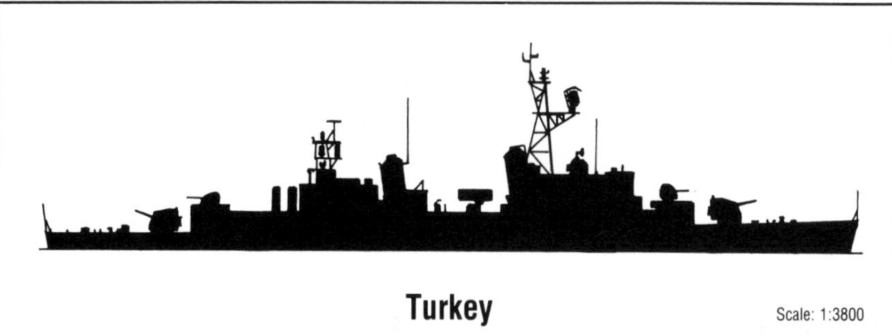
Turkey
Scale: 1:3800

D354
D354

Number in class: 1

KOCATEPE D354 1974 (1945)

Destroyer

Gearing (FRAM II) Class

Specifications and Technical Data

Displacement, tonnes: 3,480 full load
Dimensions, metres (feet): 119 × 12.6 × 5.8 (390.5 × 41.2 × 19)
Guns: 2 × 2 127 mm, one fore, one aft; 2 × 2 40 mm on each beam amidships; 1 × 2 35 mm aft
Torpedoes: 2 × 3 324 mm Mk32 for Mk 46 ASW LWT
ASW Weapons: 1 × Mk 15 Hedgehog foreward, 1 × 9 charge depth charge rack at stern
Sonar: SQS 23 hull-mounted medium-frequency active
Radar: SPS 40 E/F band air search, SPS 10 G band surface search, I band navigation, Mk 25 fire control
Machinery: 2 × sets geared turbines, 2 × shafts, 60,000 hp, 4 × boilers
Speed, knots: 32
Range, nautical miles: 4,800 at 15 knots
Complement: 274

Formerly USS *Norris* built by Bethlehem Steel, San Pedro, California, being laid down in August 1944, launched in February 1945 and commissioned in June the same year. In 1949 she was converted into an escort destroyer (DDE) with B gun mount replaced by a trainable Hedgehog ASW weapon. She received an austere FRAM II conversion and was sold to Turkey in July 1974 for cannibalisation to keep Turkey's other destroyers in service. Later that month, however, her sister ship, the former USS *Harwood* which had been sold to Turkey the previous year, was bombed in error by the Turkish Air Force during the invasion of Cyprus. It was decided, therefore, to replace her with the *Norris* which was prepared for service with two extra single 40 mm anti-aircraft guns-mounted on the former drone helicopter deck. These guns were supplemented by two twin 40 mm mountings on each beam between the funnels added in 1977. The two single 40 mm mounts were replaced by one twin Oerlikon 35 mm mounting in 1980. During this refit the SPS 40 air search radar was fitted in place of the previous SPS 6D. The main difference between *Kocatepe* and the other Turkish 'Gearings' is her lack of ASROC.

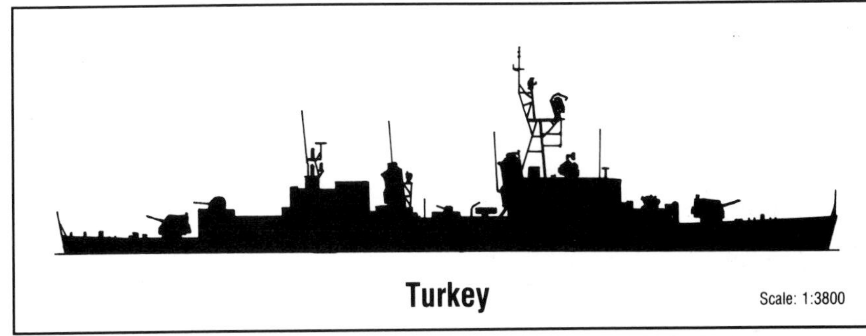

Turkey Scale: 1:3800

Photograph: *Kocatepe* (H Ehlers/USNI)

D356
D356

Number in class: 1

ZAFER D356 1972 (1945)

Specifications and Technical Data

Destroyer

Allen M. Sumner (FRAM II) Class

Displacement, tonnes: 3,300 full load
Dimensions, metres (feet): 114.8 × 12.5 × 5.8 (376.5 × 40.9 × 19)
Guns: 3 × 2 127 mm, two forward, one aft; 2 × 2 40 mm amidships; 1 × 2 35 mm aft
Torpedoes: 2 × 3 324 mm Mk32 for Mk 46 ASW LWT
ASW Weapons: 2 × Mk 15 Hedgehog on each beam beside bridge, 1 × 9 charge depth charge rack at stern
Sonar: SQS 29 hull-mounted high-frequency active
Radar: SPS 37 B/C band air search, SPS 10 G band surface search, Mk 25 I/J band fire control
Machinery: 2 × sets geared steam turbines, 2 × shafts, 60,000 hp, 4 × boilers
Speed, knots: 33
Range, nautical miles: 4,300 at 11 knots
Complement: 275

Photograph: *Zafer* 1984 (USNI)

The 'Allen M. Sumner' class destroyers were designed in 1942 in the first year of the Pacific War in order to combine, in an interim design, the new 5-inch twin dual-purpose gun mounting and the existing 'Fletcher' class hull. A heavy light-anti-aircraft armament was fitted. Range proved inadequate and after 58 units the class was replaced by the longer, but otherwise similar, 'Gearings'. *Zafer* was on of the last of the 'Sumner' class to be built, being originally laid down as the USS *Hugh Purvis* at the Federal Shipbuilding Yard, Kearny, New Jersey on 23 May 1944. She was launched in 17 December of that year and commissioned on 1 March 1945. Like many, but not all, of her sisters she was given an austere FRAM II conversion in the 1960s. This included limited rehabilitation of the hull and machinery, plus some modernisation of weapons and electronics, including fitting a modern longer-range active/passive sonar. *Hugh Purvis* was then used as trials ship both with the unsuccessful drone helicopter DASH weapons delivery system, and for planar passive sonar arrays. She was purchased from the United States in February 1972. She has been further modernised by them with a modern light gun armament. Two twin 40 mm mounts were added amidships in 1977, and in 1979 a twin 35 mm Oerlikon mounting replaced two single 40 mm Bofors guns formerly mounted by the Turks on the old DASH deck. *Zafer* with her full original gun armament retains some capability in the anti-surface and shallow water anti-submarine role.

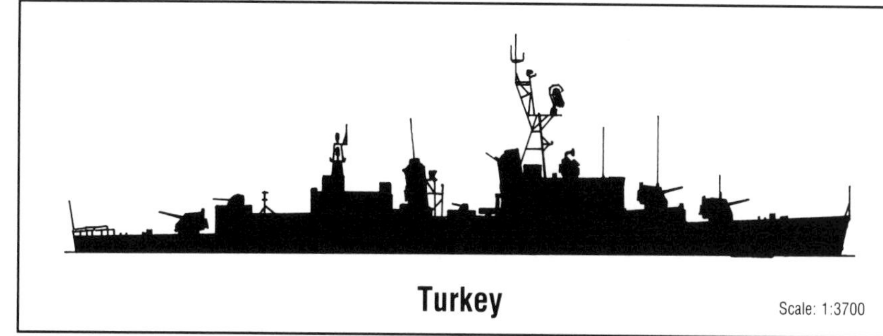

Turkey

Scale: 1:3700

DM357
DM357

Number in class: 1

MUAVENET DM357 1971 (1944)

Robert H. Smith Class

Specifications and Technical Data

Displacement, tonnes: 3,375 full load
Dimensions, metres (feet): 114.8 × 12.5 × 5.8 (376.5 × 40.9 × 19)
Guns: 3 × 2 127 mm, two forward, one aft; 1 × 2 76 mm aft; 2 × 4 40 mm on each beam abaft second funnel; 2 × 2 40 mm on either beam abaft bridge
Torpedoes: 2 × 3 324 mm Mk32 for Mk 46 ASW LWT
ASW Weapons: 2 × Mk 10 Hedgehog on eitherside of bridge, 1 × 9 charge depth charge rack at stern
Sonar: QCU or QHB hull-mounted high-frequency active
Radar: SPS 40 E/F band air search, SPS 10 G band surface search, Mk 25 and Mk 34 I/J band fire control
Machinery: 2 sets geared turbines, 2 × shafts, 60,000 hp, 4 × boilers
Speed, knots: 34
Range, nautical miles: 4,600 at 15 knots
Complement: 274

Photograph: *Muavenet* 1984 (H Ehlers/USNI)

The 'Robert H. Smith' class was a subgroup of the 'Allen M. Sumner' class converted into minelayers following combat experience in the Solomon Islands. Two were retained in commission in the 1950s and one of these, the USS *Gwin*, after being laid up in the 1960s, was chosen to be transferred to Turkey, a nation with a considerable requirement for mine warfare capability. She was modernised with new fire control before transfer in October 1971, but retained her World War II anti-submarine and general weapons fit. The Turks gave her a further modernisation in 1982-3 with a new air search radar and 76 mm rather than 40 mm guns aft. Eighty mines can be carried on rails leading back to the stern. She was built by the Bethlehem Steel Corporation, San Pedro, California being laid down on 31 October 1943 and launched on 9 April 1944.

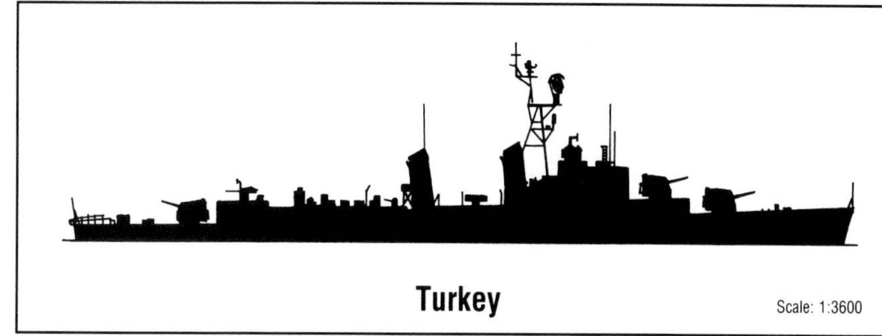

Turkey

Scale: 1:3600

D360

Number in class: 4

GELIBOLU D360 1983 (1962)
GEMLIK D361 1983 (1961)
ex-LÜBECK D362 1988 (1963)
ex-BRAUNSCHWEIG 1989 (1964)

Specifications and Technical Data

Displacement, tonnes: 2,970 full load
Dimensions, metres (feet): 109.9 × 11 × 5.1 (360.5 × 36.1 × 16.7)
Guns: 2 × 1 100 mm, one forward, one aft; 2 × 2 and 2 × 1 40 mm twin mounts fore and aft; single 40 mm guns on each beam aft
Torpedoes: 4 × 1 533 mm for ASW HWT
ASW Weapons: 2 × 4-barrelled 375 mm rocket launchers
Sonar: PAE CWE high/medium-frequency hull-mounted active
Radar: DA 08 F band air/surface search, Kelvin Hughes I band navigation, M 44 I/J band 100 mm fire control, M 45 I/J band 40 mm fire control
Machinery: 2 × Brown Boveri gas turbines, 26,000 hp, 4 × MAN diesels, 12,000 hp, 2 × shafts
Speed, knots: 28
Range, nautical miles: 3,000 at 18 knots
Complement: 210

Photograph: *Gelibolu* 1984 (USNI)

Former German frigates whose heavy gun armament, shallow-water ASW capacity and minelaying capability (80 mines) suit Turkish requirements. *Gemlik* suffered a serious fire and may be cannibalised for spares for the rest of the class. These ships had a somewhat chequered career in German service suffering structural defects in their early days. They were built by H.C. Stulcken of Hamburg, being laid down respectively on 15 December and 15 April 1958, 28 October 1959 and 28 July 1960. Launch dates were 24 October 1959, 21 March 1959, 23 July 1960 and 3 February 1962.

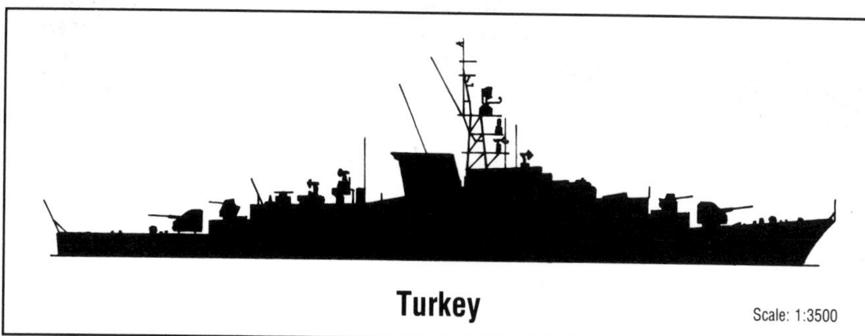

Turkey

Scale: 1:3500

D359
D359

Specifications and Technical Data

Number in class: 2

BERK D358 1972
PEYK D359 1975

Berk Class

Displacement, tonnes: 1,950 full load
Dimensions, metres (feet): 95 × 11.8 × 5.5 (311.7 × 38.7 18.1)
Guns: 2 × 2 76 mm, one forward, one aft
Torpedoes: 2 × 3 324 mm Mk32 for Mk 46 ASW LWT
ASW Weapons: 2 × Mk 11 Hedgehog on each beam, 1 × 9 charge depth charge rack at stern
Sonar: SQS 29/31 hull-mounted high-frequency active
Radar: SPS 30 E/F band air search, SPS 10 G band surface search, I band navigation, Mk 34 fire control
Machinery: 3 × Fiat-Tosi Type 3-016-RSS diesels, 1 × shaft, 24,000 hp
Speed, knots: 25

These were the first warships of any size built in Turkey, being laid down at the Gulcuk Naval Shipyard on 9 March 1967 and 18 January 1968. They were launched on 25 June 1971 and 7 June 1972. The design is based on that of the USS *Claud Jones*, a very simple destroyer escort designed for mass production in case of war in the 1950s. These ships were not successful in the US Navy in any peacetime role except electronic intelligence gathering, but, as an exceptionally simple design, they were suitable for Turkey's first essay in frigate construction. They differed from the original American ships in having Italian machinery and one funnel instead of two. Their gun armament was also a little heavier. Since being delivered they have had their sonar upgraded although they only remain suitable for very short-range shallow-water operations. The ships carry a helicopter deck which allows them to act as a forward platform for AB 212 ASW dipping sonar helicopters.

Photograph: *Peyk* (Selçuk Emre/USNI)

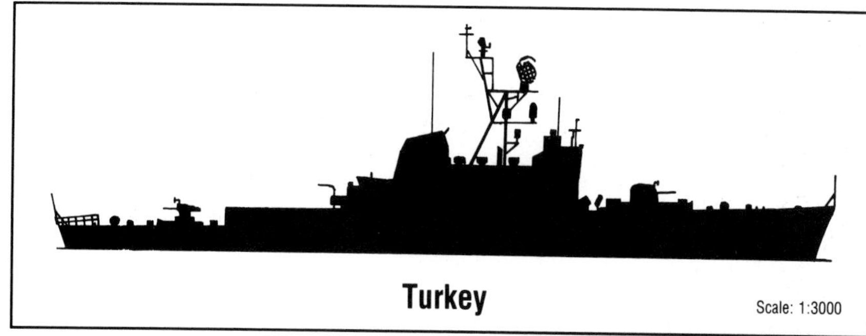

F230

Specifications and Technical Data

Number in class: 10

NORFOLK F230 1989
ARGYLL F231 1991
LANCASTER F232 1991
MARLBOROUGH F233 1990
IRON DUKE F234 1992
MONMOUTH F235 1992
MONTROSE F236 1993
WESTMINSTER
NORTHUMBERLAND
RICHMOND

Duke (Type 23) Class

Displacement, tonnes: 3,850 full load
Dimensions, metres (feet): 133 × 16.1 × 5.5 (436.2 × 52.8 × 18)
Aircraft: 2 × Lynx helicopters
Missiles: SSM: 2 × 4 Harpoon forward
SAM: 32 × Seawolf GWS 26 vertical launch forward
Guns: 1 × 1 114 mm forward, 2 × 2 30 mm on each beam
Torpedoes: 2 × 2 324 mm fixed for Stingray ASW LWT
Sonar: 2031Z towed array, 2050 bow-mounted medium-frequency active
Radar: 996 3D E/F band air/surface search, 1007 I band navigation, 911 I band fire control
Action Information Organisation: SSCS
Machinery: 2 × Rolls-Royce Spey SM1A gas turbines, 34,000 hp, 4 × Paxman Velenta 12 RPA 200 CZ diesels, 7,000 hp, 2 × GEC 1.5mw electric motors, 2 × shafts
Speed, knots: 28
Range, nautical miles: 7,800 at 15 knots
Complement: 146

Originally projected in 1981 as little more than tugs for towed array sonar, these vessels have grown into small fleet ASW destroyers of the minimum size required for operation with the ASW Striking Force of the NATO Striking Fleet. The ships have been made especially silent with innovative CODLAG combined diesel electric and gas turbine propulsion systems. Maximum speed on diesel electric propulsion is 15 knots. The Lynx helicopters will be replaced by the large Merlin helicopter when this becomes available in the 1990s. This will allow the frigates to prosecute their own long-range contacts. The main problem with these ships is the failure of their intended computerised command system CACS 4. The main reason for this was the expansion in the ships' capabilities and the extra strain this put on the original system. A new surface ship command system (SSCS) is being developed for the Type 23s, but the contract was only signed in mid-1989, and the first seven ships will commission without any computerised action information organisation. This will cause a serious degradation in their effectiveness and they will not be fully front line units. In 1989 the British Government announced orders for the three newest members of the class from Swan Hunter, Wallsend, builders of **F233**.

Tenders for the construction of up to four more members may be announced in 1990, and at least two further members of the class are expected later. The other six initial vessels are being built by Yarrow in Glasgow. Yarrow acted as lead shipbuilder for the class playing a major role in its detailed design.

Photograph: *Norfolk* (Yarrow Shipbuilders)

United Kingdom

Scale: 1:4200

F85

Cornwall (Type 22 Batch 3) Class

Number in class: 4

CORNWALL F99 1988
CUMBERLAND F85 1989
CAMPBELTOWN F86 1989
CHATHAM F87 1990

Specifications and Technical Data

Displacement, tonnes: 4,900 full load
Dimensions, metres (feet): 148.1 × 14.8 × 6.4 (485.9 × 48.5 × 21)
Aircraft: 1 × Sea King helicopter
Missiles: SSM: 2 × 4 Harpoon abaft bridge
SAM: 2 × 6 Seawolf GWS 25 MOD 3
Guns: 1 × 1 114 mm forward, 1 × 1 30 mm Goalkeeper CIWS abaft bridge, 2 × 1 30 mm on each beam
Torpedoes: 2 × 3 324 mm STWS 2 for Mk 46 or Stingray ASW LWT
Sonar: 2031Z towed array, 2016 hull-mounted low-frequency active
Radar: 967/968 D/E band air/surface search, 1006 I band navigation, 911 I band Seawolf fire control
Action Information Organisation: CACS 5
Machinery: 2 × Rolls-Royce Spey SM1A gas turbines, 37,540 hp, 2 × Rolls-Royce Tyne RM3C gas turbines, 9,700 hp, 2 × shafts
Speed, knots: 30
Range, nautical miles: 4,500 at 18 knots
Complement: 250

These final versions of the Type 22 design incorporate all the lessons of the Falklands War. They are fleet ASW destroyers rather than frigates and can act as flagships if required. Up to two Lynx helicopters may be carried as an alternative to the Sea King. Both types will be replaced by the Merlin in the 1990s. The ships have a full countermeasures suite with Guardian ESM and four Sea Gnat 6-barrelled chaff and flare launchers. A Type 182 towed torpedo decoy can be deployed. The 2016 sonar is being upgraded to 2050 standard. **F99** and **F85** were built by Yarrow, Glasgow, being launched respectively on 14 October 1985 and 21 June 1986. **F86** was built by Cammell Laird, Birkenhead being launched on 7 October 1987 and **F87** was constructed by Swan Hunter, Wallsend being launched on 20 January 1988. These four ships together form the 8th Frigate Squadron based at Devonport.

United Kingdom

Scale: 1:4600

Photograph: *Cumberland* (HM Steele/Naval Forces)

F94
BRAVE

Specifications and Technical Data

Number in class: 10

BROADSWORD F88 1979
BATTLEAXE F89 1980
BRILLIANT F90 1981
BRAZEN F91 1982
BOXER F92 1984
BEAVER F93 1984
BRAVE F94 1986
LONDON F95 1987
SHEFFIELD F96 1988
COVENTRY F98 1988

Broadsword (Type 22 Batches 1 and 2) Class

Displacement, tonnes: 4,400 (F88-91) 4,800 (remainder) full load
Dimensions, metres (feet): 131.2 (F88-91) 145 (F92-3) 146.5 (remainder) × 14.8 × 6(F88-91) 6.4 (remainder) (430/485.8/490.5 × 48.5 × 19.9/21)
Aircraft: 2 × Lynx or (F94 onwards) 1 × Sea King.
Missiles: SSM: 4 × 1 Exocet forward
SAM: 2 × 6 Seawolf GWS 25
Guns: 2 × 2 30 mm on each beam amidships, provision for 2 × 1 20 mm
Torpedoes: 2 × 3 324 mm STWS 2 for Mk 46 or Stingray ASW LWT
Sonar: (except F88-91) 2031Z towed array, (all) 2016 hull-mounted medium-frequency active
Radar: 967/968 D/E band air/surface search, 1006 I band navigation, 911 I band Seawolf fire control
Action Information Organisation: CAAIS (F88-91), CACS 1 (remainder)
Machinery: 2 × Rolls-Royce Olympus TM3B, 54,600hp (F88-93); Spey SM1C, 48,000hp, (F94); Spey SM1A 37,540 hp (rest); 2 × Rolls-Royce Tyne RM1C gas turbines, 9,700 hp, 2 × shafts
Speed, knots: 30
Range, nautical miles: 4,500 at 18 knots
Complement: (F88-91) 222, (remainder) 273

Originally intended as 'Leander' class frigate replacements these ships emerged as large and capable fleet ASW destroyers. The second batch of vessels, from *Boxer* onwards, was lengthened which improved seakeeping. The vessels are very well laid-out internally. *Broadsword* and *Battleaxe* were originally built with differently designed funnels, but these are being replaced on refit with the more elegant later design. *Broadsword* and *Brilliant* fought in the Falklands War where their Seawolf SAMs proved most effective. All but **F96** and **F98** were built by Yarrow in Glasgow. Launch dates were, **F88** 12 May 1976, **F89** 18 May 1977, **F90** 15 December 1978, **F91** 4 March 1980, **F92** 17 June 1981, **F93** 8 May 1982, **F94** 19 November 1983, and **F95** 27 October 1984. The final pair, replacements for Type 42 destroyers of the same name sunk in the Falklands War were built by Swan Hunter at Wallsend. **F96** was launched on 26 March 1986 and **F98** on 8 April 1986. Only the lengthened Batch 2 vessels are being fitted with towed array which greatly enhances their effectiveness in ASW Striking Force operations. All units, however, are having their 2016 active sonars upgraded to 2050 standard. Normally a single Lynx helicopter is carried by all ships but Sea Kings can be embarked in **F94** onwards. **F88-91** form the 2nd Frigate Squadron and the rest of the class the 1st Frigate Squadron, both based at Devonport.

Photograph: *Brave* (HM Steele/Naval Forces)
Silhouette: Batch 1

United Kingdom

Scale: 1:4300

D23

Bristol (Type 82) Class

Number in class: 1

BRISTOL D23 1973

Specifications and Technical Data

Displacement, tonnes: 7,100 full load
Dimensions, metres (feet): 154.5 × 16.8 × 5.2 (507 × 55 × 16.8)
Missiles: SAM: 1 × 2 Sea Dart GWS 30 aft, 40 missiles
Guns: 1 × 1 114 mm forward, 2 × 2 30 mm on each beam, 2 × 1 BMARC 20 mm on each beam by after funnel, 2 × 1 Oerlikon 20 mm on each beam by fore funnel
Sonar: 184P hull-mounted medium-frequency active, 162M hull-mounted high-frequency classification
Radar: 1022 D band air search, 992R E/F band surface search, 1006 I band navigation, 909 I/J band fire control
Action Information Organisation: ADAWS 2
Machinery: 2 × sets geared steam turbines, 30,000 hp, 2 × Rolls-Royce Olympus TM1A gas turbines, 30,000 hp, 2 × shafts, 2 × boilers
Speed, knots: 30
Range, nautical miles: 5,000 at 18 knots
Complement: 397

Originally projected in the 1960s as escorts for the new generation of British aircraft carriers, the rest of the class was cancelled in 1967 in favour of a more cost-effective destroyer design. The Type 82s had themselves been conceived of as cheaper fleet escorts, being based on an enlarged 'Leander' class frigate concept with improved radar and the new, more compact Sea Dart missile system. The design grew, however, with the addition of gas turbine supplementary propulsion of equivalent power to the steam plant and the ship turned out larger than that of its 'County' class predecessor. Surprisingly, unlike the 'Counties', space could not be found for a helicopter and *Bristol* only has a deck landing platform aft. The original ASW armament was the Australian Ikara missile system mounted forward, but this has since been removed. *Bristol* spent her early days as a trial ship for her new systems and ran for some time on gas turbines alone after a serious engine room fire. She was refitted as a flagship in 1979-80 and was originally to be disposed of in 1984. Instead, however, she was refitted as Dartmouth Training Ship in 1984-6. She therefore has a slightly reduced war role, but if required she can act as the flagship of Flag Officer First Flotilla. *Bristol* was built by Swan Hunter of Wallsend and was laid down on 15 November 1967 and launched on 30 June 1969. She is fitted with the full range of data links, 10, 11 and 14.

Photograph: *Bristol* 1989 (HM Steele/Naval Forces)

United Kingdom

Scale: 1:4900

D91

Destroyers

Sheffield (Type 42) Class

Number in class: 11

BIRMINGHAM D86 1976
NEWCASTLE D87 1978
GLASGOW D88 1979
EXETER D89 1980
SOUTHAMPTON D90 1981
NOTTINGHAM D91 1983
LIVERPOOL D92 1981
MANCHESTER D95 1982
GLOUCESTER D96 1985
EDINBURGH D97 1985
YORK D98 1985

Specifications and Technical Data

Displacement, tonnes: 4,100 full load; (D95-8) 4,775 full load
Dimensions, metres (feet): 125 × 14.3 × 5.8 (412 × 47 × 19); (D95-8) 141.1 × 14.9 × 5.8 (462.8 × 49 × 19)
Aircraft: 1 × Lynx helicopter
Missiles: SAM: 1 × 2 Sea Dart GWS 30 forward, 22 missiles
Guns: 1 × 1 114 mm forward, 2 × 1 Vulcan Phalanx 20 mm CIWS on each beam, 2 × 1 BMARC 20 mm aft on each beam, 2 × 1 20 mm Oerlikon in bridge wings
Torpedoes: 2 × 3 324 mm STWS 2 for Mk 46 or Stingray ASW LWT
Sonar: 184P or 2050 hull-mounted medium frequency active, 162M hull-mounted classification
Radar: 1022 D band air search, 992 or 996 E/F band surface search, 1006 I band navigation, 909 or 9091 I/J band fire control
Action Information Organisation: ADAWS 4
Machinery: 2 × Rolls-Royce Olympus TN3B gas turbines, 50,000 hp, 2 × Rolls-Royce Tyne RM1C gas turbines, 9,700 hp, 2 × shafts
Speed, knots: 29, (D95-8) 30 plus
Range, nautical miles: 4,000 at 18 knots
Complement: 253

The Type 42s were designed at the end of the 1960s to be a more cost effective answer to the problem of providing a fleet area defence anti-air warfare escort. The last four were lengthened which improved their seakeeping. These four ships have required hull strengthening. A great deal has been crammed into a relatively small space, but in combat terms they are effective enough both in their primary anti-air and secondary ASW roles. Their ASW potential is significantly enhanced when fitted with the new 2050 sonar. CIWS fills a significant point defence gap which contributed to the loss in action of two ships of this class in the Falklands War, *Sheffield* and *Coventry*. The lengthened ships will receive Lightweight Seawolf in the 1990s. The Sea Dart missiles can double in the surface-to-surface role. Builders for the class were: Cammell Laird, Birkenhead, **D86** launched July 1973, **D92** September 1980, **D97** April 1983; Swan Hunter, Wallsend, **D87** April 1975, **D88** April 1976, **D89** April 1978, **D98** June 1982; Vickers, Barrow, **D108** February 1974, **D95** November 1980; Vosper Thornycroft, **D90**, January 1979, **D91** February 1980, **D96** November 1982. The ships carry a comprehensive ESM/ECM suite with UAA-1 ESM, 670 jammers, either Corvus or Shield trainable chaff launchers and SRBOC 6-tubed fixed chaff/flare launchers. The Type 42s are due to be replaced at the turn of the century by new asir defence frigates.

Photograph: *Nottingham* (HM Steele)
Silhouette: D95-D98

F171

Amazon (Type 21) Class

Specifications and Technical Data

Number in class: 6

AMAZON F169 1974
ACTIVE F171 1977
AMBUSCADE F172 1975
ARROW F173 1976
ALACRITY F174 1977
AVENGER F185 1978

Displacement, tonnes: 3,600 full load
Dimensions, metres (feet): 117 × 12.7 × 5.9 (384 × 41.7 × 19.5)
Aircraft: 1 × Lynx helicopter
Missiles: SSM: 4 × 1 MM 38 Exocet forward
SAM: 1 × 4 Seacat GWS 24 aft
Guns: 1 × 1 114 mm forward, 2 or 4 × 1 20 mm
Torpedoes: 2 × 3 324 mm STWS 2 for Mk 46 or Stingray ASW LWT
Sonar: 184P hull-mounted medium-frequency active, 162M hull-mounted classification
Radar: 992R E/F band air/surface search, 1006 I band navigation, 912 I/J band fire control
Action Information Organisation: CAAIS
Machinery: 2 × Rolls-Royce Olympus TM3B gas turbines, 50,000 hp, 2 × Rolls-Royce Tyne RM1C gas turbines, 9,700 hp, 2 × shafts
Speed, knots: 30
Range, nautical miles: 4,000 at 17 knots
Complement: 175

These vessels were designed by a Vosper Thornycroft/Yarrow consortium in order to provide a relatively cheap unit to replace the eight Second Rate diesel-powered frigates paid off in the 1970s. The result was a handsome class with high performance, popular with its crews. During the 1980s, however, various problems made their appearance. The ships proved vulnerable both to accident and battle damage, and two, *Ardent* and *Antelope*, were sunk in the Falklands War. Operations in heavy weather conditions strained the structures and severe cracks appeared in the upper decks. This has necessitated strengthening being added to the ships' sides. Extra ballast to improve stability has caused an increase in full load displacement from the original figure of 3,250 tonnes. *Amazon* and *Active* were built by Vosper Thornycroft at Woolston and were launched on 26 April 1971 and 23 November 1972. The other four were built by Yarrow in Glasgow and were launched on 18 January 1973 (*Ambuscade*), 5 February 1974 (*Arrow*), 18 September 1974 (*Alacrity*) and 20 November 1975 (*Avenger*). The ships carry UAA-1 ESM and Corvus chaff launchers. The 182 towed torpedo decoy is also available. It was originally intended to mount Seawolf in these ships, but the mounting proved too heavy and an advanced Seacat system was mounted instead. Work is being carried out on these ships to extend their life to about 22 years. This includes the addition of transom flaps to improve propulsive efficiency and reduce both hull resistance and noise. *Avenger* was the first to complete this modernisation in 1988.

Photograph: *Active* (HM Steele/Naval Forces)

United Kingdom

Scale: 1:3700

F60

Leander (Batch 3) Class

Number in class: 7

ANDROMEDA F57 1968
HERMIONE F58 1969
JUPITER F60 1969
SCYLLA F71 1970
CHARYBDIS F75 1969
ACHILLES F12 1970
ARIADNE F72 1973

Specifications and Technical Data

Note: Data refers only to **F57, 58, 60, 71, 75**
Displacement, tonnes: 3,100 full load
Dimensions, metres (feet): 113.4 × 13.1 × 5.5 (372 × 43 × 18)
Aircraft: 1 × Lynx helicopter
Missiles: SSM: 2 × 2 MM 38 Exocet
SAM: 1 × 6 Seawolf GWS 25 forward, 32 missiles
Guns: 2 or (F58,75) 3 × 1 20 mm
Torpedoes: 2 × 3 324 mm STWS 2 for Mk 46 or Stingray ASW LWT
Sonar: 2016 hull-mounted medium-frequency active, 162M classification
Radar: 967/968 D/E band air/surface search, 1006 I band navigation, 910 I/J band Seawolf fire control
Action Information Organisation: CAAIS
Machinery: 2 sets geared steam turbines, 30,000 hp, 2 × boilers
Speed, knots: 28
Range, nautical miles: 4,000 at 15 knots
Complement: 260

The Batch 3 (or broad-beamed) 'Leanders' were all originally to have been modernised to give them a capability comparable to the Type 22. The expense of this conversion caused it to be abandoned in the 1981 Defence Review with only the first five ships converted. Conversion completion dates were, **F57** December 1980, **F58** June 1983, **F60** October 1983, **F71** December 1984, **F75** August 1982. The remaining five ships retained their original armament of twin 127 mm mount forward, Mk 10 ASW mortar aft and Wasp weapons delivery helicopter. Their sensors including Type 184 hull-mounted sonar and 966 air search radar were also unchanged. Three of these ships have now been paid off and the other two, **F12** and **F72** (both built by Yarrow in Glasgow), are now only useful for training as the Wasp helicopter has been phased out. They form the Dartmouth Training Squadron along with the destroyer HMS *Bristol*. The five conversions remain highly capable vessels and were used side by side with later types in the Gulf. Builders were, *Andromeda* Portsmouth Dockyard launched 24 May 1967, *Hermione* Stephen, Glasgow 26 April 1967, *Jupiter* Yarrow, Glasgow 4 September 1967, *Scylla* Devonport Dockyard 8 August 1968 and *Charybdis* Harland Wolff, Belfast 28 February 1968. In many respects it was a pity that this conversion programme was halted as the newer hulls have had to be disposed of first. Nevertheless, it is likely that these ships will be kept in service as long as possible. They are in many ways 'mini Type 22s' and can be deployed accordingly. *Jupiter* was trials ship for the improved 2050 sonar.

Photograph: *Jupiter* (Ferranti/Naval Forces)

F28

Number in class: 7

CLEOPATRA F28 1966
SYRIUS F40 1966
PHOEBE F42 1966
ARGONAUT F56 1967
MINERVA F45 1979
DANAE F47 1967
PENELOPE F127 1963

Leander (Batch 2) Class

Specifications and Technical Data

Displacement, tonnes: 3,200 full load
Dimensions, metres (feet): 113.4 × 12.5 × 5.8 (372 × 41 × 19)
Aircraft: 1 × Lynx helicopter
Missiles: SSM: 2 × 2 MM 38 Exocet forward
SAM: 2 or (F45, F47, F127) 3 × Seacat GWS 21
Guns: (F45, F47, F127) 2 × 1 40 mm either side of foremast, (all) 2 × 1 20 mm
Torpedoes: 2 × 3 324 mm STWS 1 for Mk 46 ASW LWT (being removed)
Sonar: (F28, F40, F42, F56) 2031I towed array, (all) 184P hull-mounted medium-frequency active, 162M hull-mounted classification
Radar: (F45, F47, F127) 966 A band air search, (all) 994 E/F band air/surface search, 1006 I band navigation, 903/904 Seacat fire control
Action Information Organisation: CAAIS
Machinery: 2 × sets geared steam turbines, 30,000 hp, 2 × shafts, 2 × boilers
Speed, knots: 28
Range, nautical miles: 4,000 at 15 knots
Complement: 266 or (F45, F47, F127) 248

The Batch 2 'Leander' class frigates are those of the original design that were converted to carry Exocet missiles rather than Ikara ASW sytems (all the latter are now paid off). The most important are **F28**, **F40**, **F42** and **F56** which were modified from 1982 to operate the Royal Navy's first towed-array very-low-frequency passive sonar. The equipment for this at the stern required considerable reduction in top weight and the air surveillance radar was removed together with the 40 mm guns, the forward Seacat launcher. The Exocet mountings were also reduced in height. The 2031I towed arrays still give excellent results and these four ships are useful assets to the ASW Striking Force. Originally *Minerva* was to have been the final TA conversion but *Argonaut* was substituted because of the need to repair combat damage in 1982. The three other Exocet 'Leanders' are still quite useful general-purpose frigates. Indeed, despite her age, *Penelope* was repaired following serious collision damage sustained on exercise in 1988. HMS *Juno*, **F52**, was to have received an Exocet conversion but this was cancelled as a result of the 1981 Defence Review and she now serves as a disarmed non-combatant training ship. Builders for the Batch 2 'Leanders' were, Devonport Dockyard **F28** (launched 25 March 1964) and **F47** (31 October 1965), Portsmouth Dockyard **F40** (22 September 1964), Stephen, Glasgow **F42** (8 July 1964), Hawthorn Leslie, Hebburn **F56** (8 February 1966), Vickers Armstrong, Newcastle **F45** (19 December 1964) and **F127** (17 August 1962).

Photograph: *Cleopatra* (Royal Navy)
Silhouette: F45, F47 and F127

United Kingdom

Scale: 1:3500

Number in class: 1

SPRINGEREN S329 1964

Submarine

Delfinen Class

Specifications and Technical Data

Displacement, tonnes: 643 submerged
Dimensions, metres (feet): 54 × 4.7 × 4.2 (177.2 × 15.4 × 13.8)
Torpedo tubes: 4 × 533 mm forward
Sonar: Hull-mounted high-frequency search and attack
Machinery: 2 × Burmeister and Wain diesels, 2 × Brown Boveri electric motors, 1,200hp, 2 × shafts
Speed, knots: 16 surfaced and submerged
Range, nautical miles: 4,000 at 8 knots
Complement: 31

Survivor of a class of four SSCs built with US funds in the 1950s and early 1960s, *Springeren* was laid down at Copenhagen Naval Dockyard in January 1961 and was launched in April 1963, significantly later than her three sisters all of which are now stricken. Maximum diving depth is only 100 metres, half that of the German-built Type 207s being purchased from Norway to replace these boats. No reloads are carried and the four torpedoes are a mix of Swedish Type 61 wire-guided anti-surface weapons and Type 41 ASW passive homers. *Springeren's* name will transfer to the Norwegian *Kya* when the latter eventually transfers and completes modernisation.

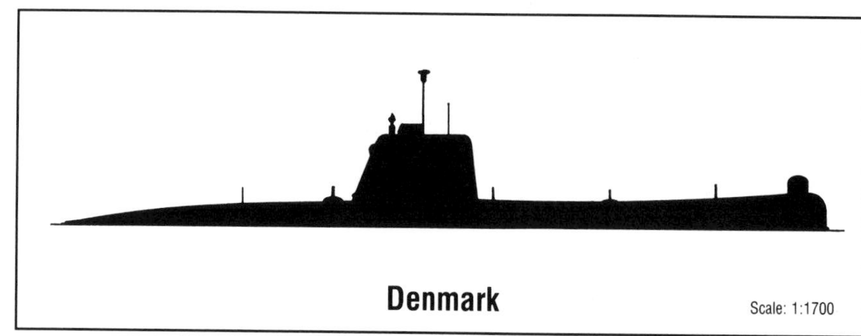

Denmark

Scale: 1:1700

Photograph: *Springeren* (van Ginderen/USNI)

S72

Number in class: 8

France	Spain
AGOSTA S620 1977	GALERNA S71 1983
BÉVÉZIERS S621 1977	SIROCO S72 1983
LA PRAYA S622 1978	MISTRAL S73 1985
OUESSANT S623 1978	TRAMONTANA S74 1986

Specifications and Technical Data

Displacement, tonnes: 1,740 submerged
Dimensions, metres (feet): 67.6 × 6.8 × 5.4 (221.7 × 22.3 × 17.7)
Torpedo tubes: 4 × 550 mm forward
Sonar: DSUV 62 (French boats only) towed array, DSUV 22 medium-frequency passive search, DUUA 2 medium-frequency active search and attack, (French boats only) DUUA 1D active search, DUUX 2 or (S73-4) DUUX 5 passive ranging
Radar: DRUA 33 I band search
Machinery: 2 × SEMT-Pielstick 320-16 PA 4 185 diesels, 3,600 hp, 1 × 3,475 kW main electric motor, 4,725hp, 123kW 'creep' motor, 1 × shaft
Speed, knots: 12 surfaced, 20 submerged
Range, nautical miles: 8,500 at 9 knots snorting, 350 at 3.5 knots on batteries submerged
Complement: 54

S620-623 French; **S71-74** Spanish. These boats are of double hull layout like earlier French submarines, but were otherwise of a completely new design. The class was originally announced in 1970 and the first boat for the French Navy was laid down in Cherbourg on 1 November 1972. She was launched on 19 October 1974. The second boat was launched in June 1975, the third in May 1976 and the fourth in October 1976. By this time two had been ordered by the Spanish Navy and they were laid down at the Bazan Yard, Cartagena in September 1977 and November 1978. Two more were ordered in June 1977 and these were laid down in May 1980 and December 1981. The four Spanish boats were launched in December 1981, November 1982, November 1983 and November 1984. About two-thirds of these submarines was produced in Spain. South Africa ordered two 'Agostas' from France, but the latter's belated adherence to the arms embargo caused their sale to Pakistan instead. The 'Agostas' carry new design tubes capable of firing both 533 mm and older 550 mm weapons. Both L5 active/passive homing torpedoes and F17 wire-guided torpedoes are carried for use against submarine and surface targets. An additional anti-surface ship option is the Exocet SM 39 missile. Twenty weapons are carried, or alternatively up to thirty-six mines. A typical mixed weapons load might be nine torpedoes and nineteen mines. Maximum diving depth is 300 metres and normal endurance nineteen days. A separate 'creep' motor can propel the submarines very quietly at 1.5 knots. The four French boats are based at Lorient.

Photograph: *Siroco* (Spanish Navy)

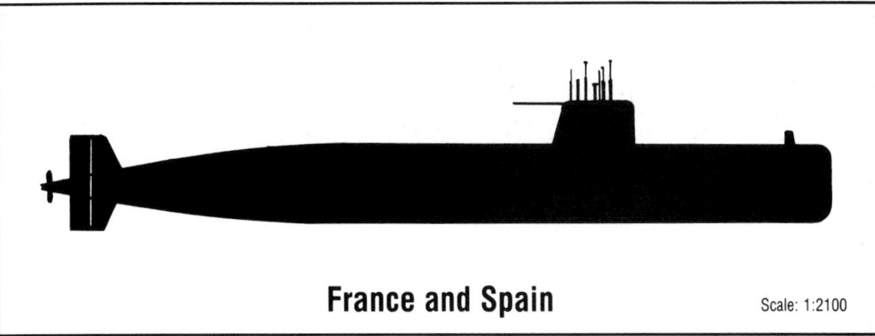

France and Spain

Scale: 1:2100

Daphné Class

Number in class: 16

France
DAPHNÉ S641 1964
DIANE S642 1964
DORIS S643 1964
FLORE S645 1964
GALATÉE S646 1964
JUNON S648 1966
VÉNUS S649 1966
PSYCHÉ S650 1969
SIRÈNE S651 1970

Portugal
ALBACORA S163 1967
BARRACUDA S164 1968
DELFIM S166 1969

Spain
DELFIN S61 1973
TONINA S62 1973
MARSOPA S63 1975
NARVAL S64 1975

Displacement, tonnes: 1,043 submerged
Dimensions, metres (feet): 57.8m × 6.8 × 4.6 (189.6 × 22.3 × 15.1)
Torpedo tubes: 12 × 550 mm, 8 forward, 4 stern
Sonar: DSUV 2 (Spanish boats DSUV 22) passive medium-frequency search and attack, DUUA 2 (*Daphné* and Portuguese boats) DUUA 1 active search and attack, DUUX 2 passive ranging
Radar: Calypso or (Spanish boats DRUA 31 or 33 A) I band search
Machinery: 2 × SEMT-Pielstick diesels, 1,300 hp, 2 × 450 kW electric motors, 2,600 hp, 2 × shafts
Speed, knots: 13.5 surfaced, 16 submerged
Range, nautical miles: 10,000 at 7 knots surfaced, 3,000 at 7 knots snorting
Complement: 45

S648-51 French; **S163-4/6** Portuguese; **S61-4** Spanish. Small 'Second Class' boats that proved popular with those countries unable to purchase military equipment elsewhere. France sold three to South Africa and three to Pakistan, and Portugal sold one of her boats to Pakistan. Of the French boats the first two were built by Dubigeon at Nantes, being launched on 20 June 1959 and 4 October 1960. The next five were built in Cherbourg Naval Dockyard and were launched in May 1960, December 1960, September 1961, May 1964 and Septmber 1964. The final pair were built at Brest Naval Dockyard both launched in June 1967. The three Portuguese boats were built by Dubigeon in France and were launched in October 1966, April, 1967 and September 1968. The four Spanish boats were built with French assistance at Bazan, Cartegena and were launched in March 1972, October 1972, March 1974 and December 1974. The boats were originally fitted with DUUA 1 active search and attack sonar, but this has been replaced in all the French boats but *Daphné* and the Portugese boats by DUUA 2. This new bow sonar is covered by a prominent dome. The French boats have had their service lives extended because of the slow completion rate of France's SSNs. **S642**, however, is already in reserve. Five of the French boats are based at Lorient and five at Toulon. The Spanish submarines are based at Cartegena. Maximum diving depth is 300 metres. The tubes, externally-mounted aft, fire E14 or E15 passive homing or L3 active homing torpedoes. There are no reloads.

Photograph: *Flore* (van Ginderen/USNI)
Silhouette: *Albacora*

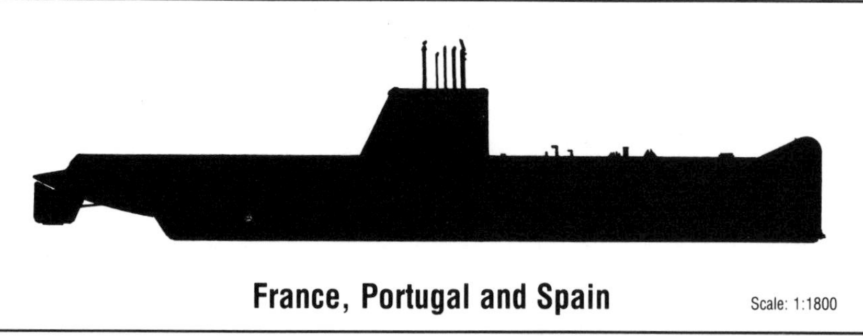

France, Portugal and Spain

Scale: 1:1800

S 199

Type 206 Class and 206A Class

Number in class: 18

U13 S192 1973
U14 S193 1973
U15 S194 1974
U16 S195 1973
U17 S196 1973
U18 S197 1973
U19 S198 1973
U20 S199 1974
U21 S170 1974
U22 S171 1974
U23 S172 1975
U24 S173 1974
U25 S174 1974
U26 S175 1975
U27 S176 1975
U28 S177 1974
U29 S178 1974
U30 S179 1975

Displacement, tonnes: 498 submerged
Dimensions, metres (feet): 48.6 × 4.6 × 4.5 (159.4 × 15.1 × 14.8)
Torpedo tubes: 8 × 660 mm forward
Sonar: 410 A4 or (206A) DBQS-21D medium-frequency search and attack, DUUX 2 passive ranging
Radar: Calypso II I band search
Action Information Organisation: HSA Mk8 or (206A) SLW 83
Machinery: 2 × MTU 12V493AZ diesels, 1,200 hp, 2 × 405 kW generators, 1 × 2,300 hp electric motor, 1 × shaft
Speed, knots: 10 surfaced, 17 submerged
Range, nautical miles: 4,500 at 5 knots surfaced
Complement: 22

Built by Howaldtswerke, Kiel and Rheinstahl Nordseewerke, Emden these boats are made of special high-tensile non-magnetic steel. Twelve of them are currently in process of modernisation to keep them in service after the year 2000. This involves fitting new DBQS-21 sonar, a modified weapons control and combat data system, new masts and periscope, and improved communications and navigation equipment. The programme is being carried out partly by Thyssen who are converting **U15**, **U22**, **U23**, **U26**, **U27** and **U30** and Howaldstwerke, the lead contractor, who are converting **U16**, **U17**, **U18**, **U25**, **U28** and **U29**. All these boats should be modernised by 1992. In this configuration they are redesignated Type 206A.

These small coastal submarines (SSCs) are extremely useful for Baltic operations, being exceptionally quiet and easy to hide. Their high-capacity batteries keep snorting to a minimum. They currently form the equipment of the Bundesmarine's front line Baltic submarine squadron, the Third, based at Eckernforde. This will progressively re-equip with the 206A boats as they become available. The submarines can also be used for minelaying with external containers for twelve mines and up to 16 more carried in the tubes at the expense of torpedoes. A reload torpedo is carried for each tube. Type 206 boats carry a mix of 533 mm DM 1 Seeal anti-ship and DM 2A1 Seeschlenge ASW wire-guided torpedoes. Modernised boats can operate the improved DM 2A3 Seehecht torpedo which can be used against both types of target.

Photograph: *U20* (USNI)

S 188

Number in class: 8

German Federal Republic
U1 S180 1967
U2 S181 1966
U9 S188 1967
U10 S189 1967
U11 S190 1968
U12 S191 1969

Denmark
NARHVALEN S320 1970
NORDKAPEREN S321 1970

Specifications and Technical Data

Displacement, tonnes: 450 submerged
Dimensions, metres (feet): U1 47.7, U2/9 43.5, U10 43.8, U11-12 45.8 S320-1 44.3 × 4.6 × 4.3 (156.5/142.7/143.7/150.3/145.3 × 15.1 × 14.1)
Torpedo tubes: 8 × 660 mm (Danish boats 553 mm) forward
Sonar: SRS M1H, S320-1 CSU 3 active/passive high-frequency search and attack,
Radar: Calypso II I band search
Machinery: 2 × MTU diesels, 1,200 hp, 2 × 405 kW generators, 1 × 1,500 hp electric motor (U1 has sixteen fuel cells 25kW), 1 × shaft
Speed, knots: 10-12 surfaced, 17 submerged
Complement: 21

The Bundesmarine boats are the surviving members of Germany's original class of post-war U-boats. **U1** and **U2**, originally launched in 1961-2, had to be totally reconstructed in normal steel due to the failure of the original non-magnetic material. The new hulls were laid down at Howaldtswerke, Kiel on 1 February 1965 and 1 September 1964 respectively. They were relaunched in February 1967 and July 1966. **U9** onwards were built with more successful non-magnetic steel. They were laid down at Howaldtswerke in December 1964, July 1965, April 1966 and September 1966. They were launched in October 1966, June 1967, February 1968 and September 1968. No reloads are carried for the torpedo tubes which are loaded through the bows. Sixteen mines can be carried in place of torpedoes. **U1** was modified in 1987 for trials with a fuel cell air-independent propulsion system. This propulsion system will be fitted to twelve new 1,200 ton Type 212 boats due to be constructed in the 1990s. These larger boats will be more full-scale SSKs than small SSCs, and will replace the six Type 205s and six unmodernised 206s that make up the First Submarine Squadron at Kiel. The Bundesmarine is considering engaging in wider ranging operations with these large boats into the Norwegian Sea and Eastern Atlantic. The two Danish boats were built under licence at the Royal Dockyard, Copenhagen. They are basically similar to the German Type 205s with a few Danish modifications. German boats carry DM 1 and DM 2A1, Danish boats Swedish Types 61 and 41 torpedoes.

Denmark and German Federal Republic

Scale: 1:1800

Photograph: *U9* (USNI)

S333
S350
S341

Submarines

Type 209 Class

Number in class: 14

Greece

GLAVKOS S110 1971
NEREUS S111 1972
TRITON S112 1972
PROTEUS S113 1972
POSYDON S116 1979
AMPHITRITE S117 1979
OKEANOS S118 1979
PONTOS S119 1980

Turkey

ATILAY S347 1975
SALDIRAY S348 1976
BATIRAY S349 1978
YILDIRAY S350 1981
DOGANAY S351 1985
DOLUNAY S352 1989

Displacement, tonnes: S110-3 1,230, remainder 1,290 submerged
Dimensions, metres (feet): S110-113 55, remainder 56.1 × 6.2 × 5.5 (180.5/184.1 × 20.3 × 17.9)
Torpedo tubes: 8 × 533 mm forward
Sonar: CSU 3 hull-mounted medium-frequency active/passive search and attack, DUUX 2 passive ranging
Radar: S110-119 Calypso II I band surface search S347-352 S 63B I band surface search
Machinery: 4 × MTU 12V493 TY60 diesels, 2,400 hp, 1 × 5,000 hp electric motor,1 × shaft
Speed, knots: 11 surfaced, 22 submerged
Range, nautical miles: 7,500 at 8 knots surfaced, 400 at 4 knots submerged
Complement: S110-S119 31, S347-352 33

S110-113 and **116-119** are Greek and **S347-352** Turkish. The boats were designed built and sold by a consortium of Ingenieurkontor (Lübeck), Ferrostaal (Essen) and Howaldtswerke (Kiel). All the Greek boats were built at Kiel, as were the first three Turkish submarines. The final three Turkish boats were, however, built with German assistance at the Golcuk Yard in Turkey. The first four Greek boats are having their sonars upgraded to the standard of the others and the Greeks plan to supplement the armament of their submarines with Sub-Harpoon anti-ship missiles. Current armament is the SST 6 wire-guided active/passive homing torpedo. Eight are carried in each tube with six reloads. Very high-capacity cooled lead-acid batteries give these small SSKs very high underwater performance. The Turks call their current boats the Type 1200, and in 1987 ordered two modified Type 1400 boats from the Golcuk Yard. The first was laid down by the Turkish Prime Minister in July 1989 with the name *Preveze*. These will be completed around 1993 and will be fitted with Sub-Harpoon missiles. They will have new KAE sonar equipment. **S352** took a long time to construct being laid down in 1981 and not launched until July 1988. Launch dates for the other Turkish boats were **S347** October 1974, **S348** February 1975, **S349** October 1977, **S350** July 1979, **S351** November 1983. Launch dates for the Greek boats were **S110** September 1970, **S111** June 1971, **S112** October 1971, **S113** February 1972, **S116** March 1978, **S117** June 1978, **S118** November 1978, **S119** March 1979.

Photograph: *Yildiray* (USNI)

Greece and Turkey

Scale: 1:1700

S333

Guppy III Class

Number in class: 3

Greece
KATSONIS S115 1973 (1946)

Turkey
IKINCI INÖNÜ S333 1973 (1945)
CANAKKALLE S341 1973 (1945)

Specifications and Technical Data

Displacement, tonnes: 2,450 submerged
Dimensions, metres (feet): 99.5 × 8.2 × 5.2 (326.5 × 27 × 17)
Torpedo tubes: 10 × 533 mm, 6 forward, 4 stern
Sonar: BQR 2B hull-mounted medium-frequency pasive search and attack, BQG4 PUFFS passive ranging
Radar: SS2A I band surface search
Machinery: S115 4 × Fairbanks-Morse 38D8-18, S331/341 General Motors 16-278A diesels, 6,400 hp, 2 × electric motors, 5,400 hp, 2 × shafts
Speed, knots: 17.5 surfaced, 15 submerged
Range, nautical miles: 10,000 at 10 knots surfaced, 95 at 5 knots submerged
Complement: 85-6

These are three of the nine American World War II type fleet submarines given extensive Guppy (Greater Underwater Propulsive Power) III conversions in the early 1960s. This was part of the FRAM (Fleet Rehabilitation and Modernisation) Programme and involved the boats being fitted with a then advanced sonar outfit including the PUFFS passive ranging equipment. The emphasis was on quiet submerged anti-submarine operations using wire-guided torpedoes. **S115** was originally laid down at Portsmouth Navy Yard in March 1945 and launched in July of the same year. The two Turkish boats were built by the Electric Boat Company of Groton, Connecticut and were both laid down in April 1944. They were launched in April 1945 (**S341**) and June 1945 (**S333**). The Guppy III conversion involved lengthening the boats by 3.6 metres to fit a plotting room. A new plastic sail improved both seakeeping on the surface and underwater streamlining. **S115**'s conversion was carried out at Pearl Harbour, **S333**'s at Charleston and **S341**'s at Philadelphia. All were completed in 1962. The original names were **S115** *Remora*, **S333** *Corporal* and **S341** *Cobbler*. All these boats were transferred to their new owners in 1973.

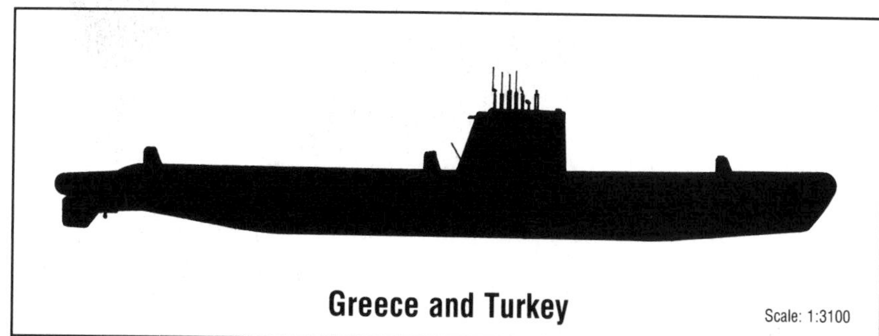

Greece and Turkey

Scale: 1:3100

Photograph: *Ikinci Inönü* (H Ehlers/USNI)

S114

Submarines
Guppy IIA Class

Specifications and Technical Data

Number in class: 6

Greece
PAPANIKOLIS S114 1972 (1944)

Turkey
BURAK REIS S335 1970 (1944)
MURAT REIS S336 1970 (1944)
ULUÇ ALI REIS S338 1973 (1944)
ÇERBE S340 1972 (1944)
BIRINCI INÖNÜ S346 1973 (1944)

Displacement, tonnes: 2,440 submerged
Dimensions, metres (feet): 93.2 × 8.2 × 5.2 (306 × 27 × 17)
Torpedo tubes: 10 × 533 mm, 6 forward, 4 stern
Sonar: BQR2B hull-mounted medium-frequency passive search and attack, Turkish boats BQS4 active, BQG3 passive ranging
Radar: I band surface search
Machinery: S114 3 × General Motors 16-278A, remainder 3 × Fairbanks-Morse 38D-1/8 diesels, 4,800 hp, 2 × electric motors, 5,400 hp, 2 × shafts
Speed, knots: 17 surfaced, 15 submerged
Range, nautical miles: 12,000 at 10 knots surfaced, 95 at 5 knots submerged
Complement: 82-4

Some of the sixteen American World War II fleet submarines given the Guppy IIA conversion in the early 1950s to improve their underwater performance and ASW capacity. The boats were streamlined and battery capacity was increased. Improved sonar was fitted and one main engine had to be removed to relocate auxiliary machinery away from the new transducers. **S340** has the earlier type stepped sail which was replaced in later conversions by a higher fin in order not to allow water to enter the boat in heavy seas. The Greek boat was built by the Manitowoc Shipbuilding Company of Wisconsin and was laid down in July 1943 and launched in December of the same year. Her original name was USS *Hardhead*. The Turkish boats were all built in the Portsmouth Navy Yard being laid down in 1943-4 and launched between January and June 1944. Their original names were **S335** *Seafox*, **S336** *Razorback*, **S338** *Thornback*, **S340** *Trutta* and **S345** *Threadfin*. *Thornback* and *Razorback* were configured on conversion as high-speed underwater targets. The Greek boat is now only used for training.

Greece and Turkey

Scale: 1:2900

Photograph: *Papanikolis* (USNI)

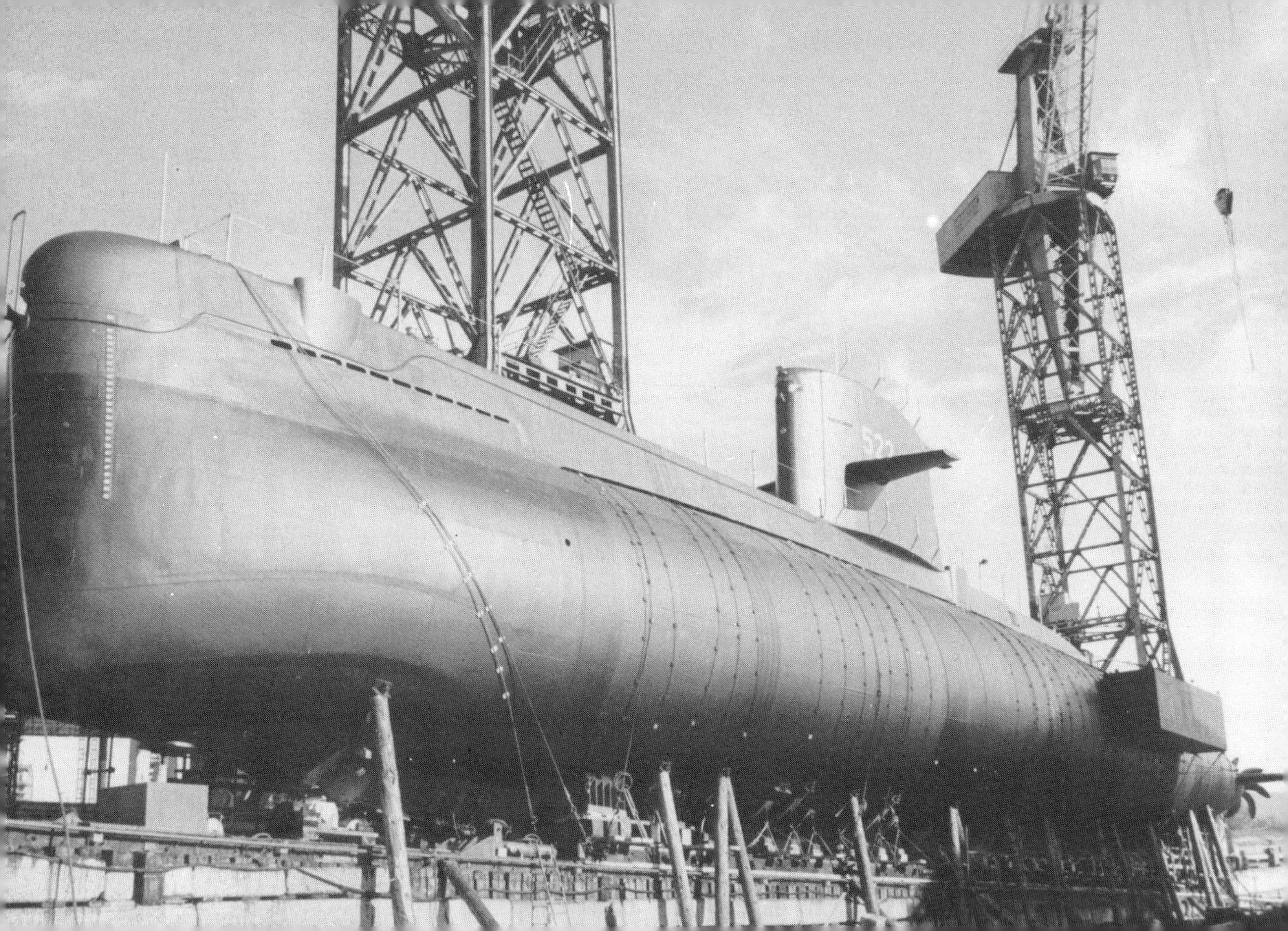

Improved Sauro Class

Number in class: 2

SALVATORE PELOSI S522 1988
GIULIANO PRINI S523 1989

Specifications and Technical Data

Displacement, tonnes: 1,680 submerged
Dimensions, metres (feet): 64.4 × 6.8 × 5.6 (211.2 × 22.3 18.4)
Torpedo tubes: 6 × 533 mm forward
Sonar: IPD 70/S combined linear passive array and active bow transducers, MD 100S passive ranging
Radar: MM/BPS 704 I band search/navigation, also attack ranging radar on periscope.
Action Information Organisation: MM/BSN 716
Machinery: 3 × GMT A210 16M diesels, 1 × 3,140 kW electric motor, 4,270 hp, 1 × shaft
Speed, knots: 11 surfaced, 19 submerged
Range, nautical miles: 11,000 at 11 knots surfaced, 250 at 4 knots submerged
Complement: 45

These boats were ordered in March 1983 from the Italcantieri Yard, Monfalcone (since renamed Fincantieri) when assembly in sections began. *Salvatore Pelosi* was launched in November 1986 and entered service in October 1987. *Guiliano Prini* was launched in December 1987 and commissioned in May 1988. The submarines were built of American HY-80 steel. The 'Improved Sauros' are slightly large compared with the original boats, being half a metre longer. They also have updated periscopes, action information and weapons control equipment. The torpedo tubes have been lengthened to take Sub-Harpoon guided missiles in addition to the normal A184 wire-guided dual-purpose homing torpedoes. The 'Improved Sauros' lack the crash dive ballast tanks of the older boats, which proved not to be necessary. Maximum normal diving depth is 300 metres and the boats have an endurance of 45 days. Two further lengthened 'Improved Sauros' were ordered in 1988, and laid down in 1989. These will displace 1,580 tons and are due to commission in 1993. Construction of this second pair will bring the Italian submarine flotilla to its planned level of twelve boats. Although well-suited to Mediterranean conditions, the 'Improved Sauros' are a little small by modern standards and a larger 2,500 tonne design is under consideration to replace the 'Toti' class in the the 1990s. This programme may well be delayed, however, by the consideration of revolutionary air-independent propulsion systems using toroidal hull construction.

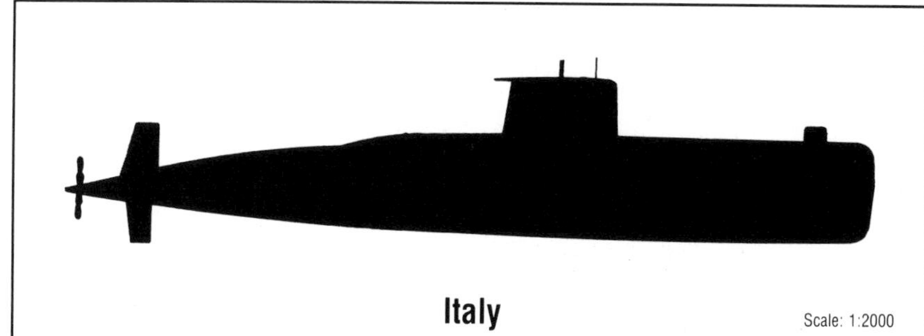

Italy

Scale: 1:2000

Photograph: *Salvatore Pelosi* 1987 (Fincantieri/Navy International)

521

Specifications and Technical Data

Number in class: 4

NAZARIO SAURO S518 1980
FECIA DI COSSATO S519 1979
LEONARDO DA VINCI S520 1981
GUGLIELMO MARCONI S521 1982

Displacement, tonnes: 1,637 submerged
Dimensions, metres (feet): 63.9 × 6.8 × 5.7 (210 × 22.5 × 18.9)
Torpedo tubes: 6 × 533 mm forward
Sonar: IPD 70/S combined linear passive array and active bow transducers, MD 100 passive ranging
Radar: MM/BPS 704 I band navigation
Action Information Organisation: SACTIS
Machinery: 3 × GMT A210 16NM diesels, 3,650 hp, 1 × 3,140 kW electric motor, 4,200 hp, 1 × shaft
Speed, knots: 11 surfaced, 19 submerged
Range, nautical miles: 11,000 at 11 knots surfaced, 250 at 4 knots submerged
Complement: 45

A class of larger Italian submarines capable of operating in hostile waters was originally projected in the late 1960s, but financial problems delayed the project, and the first boats were not actually ordered until 1972. The second pair were ordered in 1976. They were built by C.R.D.A. of Monfalcone. Launch dates were October 1976, November 1977, October 1979 and September 1980. Commissioning of the first two boats was delayed by battery problems, solved when first *Cossato* and then *Sauro* were fitted with new Swedish CGA batteries. The submarines can now maintain over 19 knots for one hour submerged. Maximum snorting speed is 12 knots and maximum normal diving depth is 300 metres. The three engines are raft-mounted in the first of three machinery spaces. The sonar system operates at a wide range of frequencies from 0.2 to 7 kHz and has surveillance, active and passive modes. Twelve torpedoes are carried, A184 dual-purpose, wire-guided active/passive homing weapons. These capable boats, fast, manoeuvrable, quiet and deep-diving are well adapted to Mediterranean conditions were Italy's first domestically produced full-size SSKs of the post-war era. They replace old second-hand American submarines in Italian service.

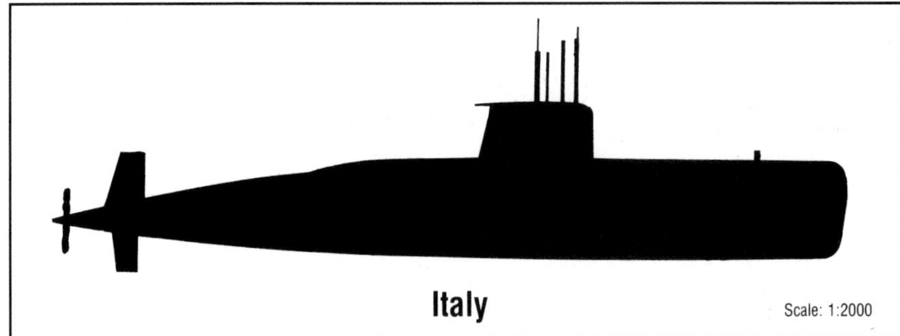

Photograph: *Gugliemo Marconi* 1984 (van Ginderen/USNI)

513

Number in class: 4

ATTILIO BAGNOLINI S505 1968
ENRICO TOTI S506 1968
ENRICO DANDOLO S513 1968
LAZZARO MOCENIGO S514 1969

Specifications and Technical Data

Displacement, tonnes: 593 submerged
Dimensions, metres (feet): 462.2 × 4.7 × 4 (151.5 × 15.4 × 13.1)
Torpedo tubes: 4 × 533 mm forward
Sonar: IPD 64 active passive medium-frequency search and attack, MD 64 passive ranging
Radar: MM/BPS 704 I band search/navigation
Action Information Organisation: IPD60/64
Machinery: 2 × Fiat/MB 820 diesels, 1 × electric motor, 2,200 hp 1 × shaft
Speed, knots: 10 surfaced, 15 submerged
Range, nautical miles: 3,000 at 5 knots surfaced
Complement: 26

These small coastal submarines (SSCs) were laid down at the C.R.D.A. yard, Monfalcone on 15 April 1965 (*Attilio Bagnolini* and *Enrico Toti*), 10 March 1967 (*Enrico Dandolo*) and 12 June 1967 (*Lazzaro Mocenigo*). Launch dates were, respectively, 26 August 1967, 12 March 1967, 16 December 1967 and 20 April 1968. Commissioning dates were 16 June 1968, 22 January 1968, 25 September 1968 and 11 January 1969. They were the first submarines to be built in Italy since 1945 and their design was changed a number of times before completion. Although small, they are quite useful in confined central Mediterranean waters. They are armed with six A184 dual-purpose wire-guided active/passive homing torpedoes, four in each tube, and a pair of reloads. These carry a 250 kilogram warhead out to 25 kilometres at 24 knots or 10 kilometres at 36 knots. The boats are useful both in anti-submarine and anti-surface ship operations. The active component of the IPD 64 sonar is housed in the prominent bow dome while the passive component is mounted a little further aft. Diving depth is 180 metres and the boats can make 15 knots for one hour on batteries submerged.

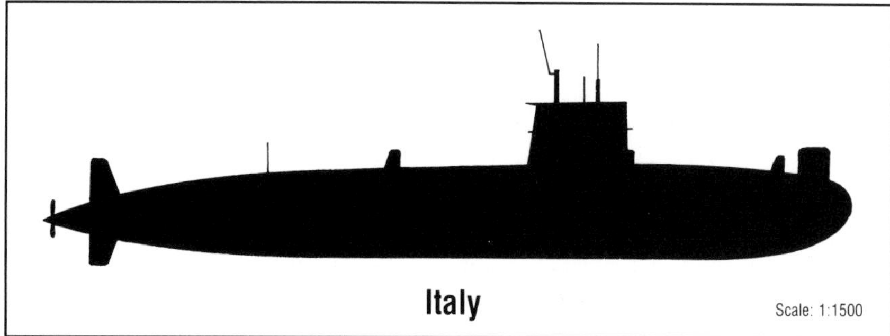

Photograph: *Enrico Dandolo* (Naval Forces)

Specifications and Technical Data

Number in class: 4

WALRUS S802 1991
ZEELEEUW S803 1989
DOLFIJN S808 1992
BRUINVIS S810 1993

Displacement, tonnes: 2,800 submerged
Dimensions, metres (feet): 67.7 × 8.4 × 6.6 (223.1 × 27.6 × 21.6)
Torpedo tubes: 4 × 533 mm forward
Sonar: 2026 towed array, Octopus hull-mounted medium-frequency active/passive search and attack
Radar: ZW 07 I band surface search
Action Information Organisation: SEWACO 8
Machinery: 3 × SEMT-Pielstick 12PA4V 200 diesels, 3,950 hp, 1 × Holec electric motor, 5,430 hp, 1 × shaft
Speed, knots: 13 surfaced, 20 submerged
Range, nautical miles: 10,000 at 9 knots snorting
Complement: 49

Photograph: *Zeeleuw* (Dutch Navy)

The procurement of these submarines has proved a long and expensive process for the Royal Dutch Navy. Originally projected in 1975, contracts on the first boats were signed in 1979. **S802** was laid down at Rotterdamse Droogdok on 11 October 1979 and **S803** on 24 September 1981. Construction was delayed by the need to lengthen the keel to house a revised diesel installation. Then, in 1986, **S802** suffered a catastrophic fire which gutted her internally. It was decided to repair her in 1987, but she will not commission until 1991 and will cost 30 per cent more than originally intended. Two more boats were ordered in 1984-5, the first was laid down on 12 June 1986 and the second on 14 April 1988. Their completion will be delayed due to the need to transfer equipment to finish **S802**. It was originally intended to build a total of six 'Walrus' class boats but the Royal Dutch Navy now plans to build two smaller 'Moray' class vessels later in the 1990s. Indeed the Dutch Navy is reconsidering its whole policy on the procurement of SSKs given the diminishing utility of passive sonar operations. Once they go to sea, however, the 'Walrus' class boats will be highly-capable vessels of their kind. They will carry a mix of twenty Mk 48 and NT 37 C/E homing torpedoes, and Sub-Harpoon anti-ship missiles. Automated systems allow the use of a reduced crew and the fire control and electronic command system is one of the most advanced of its kind. Normal maximum diving depth is 300 metres.

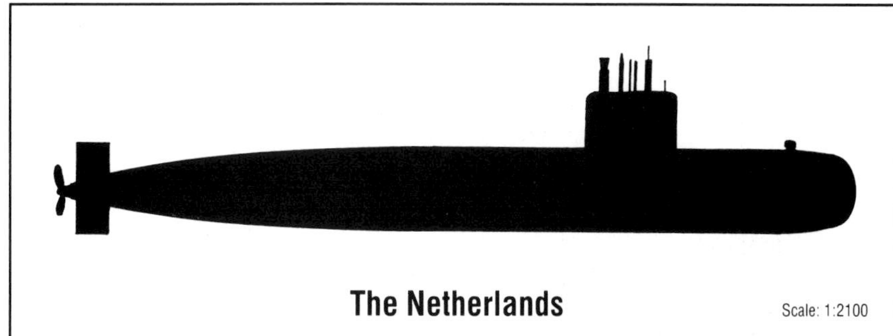

The Netherlands

Scale: 1:2100

Number in class: 2

ZWAARDVIS S806 1972
TIJGERHAAI S807 1972

Specifications and Technical Data

Displacement, tonnes: 2,640 submerged
Dimensions, metres (feet): 66 × 8.4 × 7.1 (216.5 × 27.6 × 23.3)
Torpedo tubes: 6 × 533 mm forward
Sonar: 2026 towed array, Eledone hull-mounted medium-frequency active/passive search and attack
Radar: 1001 I band surface search
Machinery: 3 × Werkspoor RUB 215X12 diesels, 4,200 hp, 1 × 3,800 kW motor, 5,100 hp, 1 × shaft
Speed, knots: 13 surfaced, 20 submerged
Range, nautical miles: 10,000 at 9 knots snorting
Complement: 67

Originally approved in the 1964 estimates to replace older American boats on loan, the 'Zwaardvis' class were built to the then advanced 'teardrop' hull layout. They are therefore built for submerged operation, either on snorkel or batteries, and are much faster underwater than on the surface. The 'Zwaardvis' design was based on that of the American 'Barbel' class boats of the late 1950s, but were modified to take Dutch equipment, and with a hull shape more like that of USS *Albacore*. *Zwaardvis* and *Tijgerhaai* (*Swordfish* and *Tigershark*) were laid down together at Rotterdamse Droogdok on 14 July 1966 being launched on 2 July 1970 and 25 May 1971. The hull is in three sections, a forward sonar and torpedo space, a three-deck central section housing the crew and operational spaces, and an after machinery space housing the three diesel engines and the electric motor. Modernisations were carried out in *Tijgerhaai* in 1988 and *Zwaardvis* in 1989-90. This involved the fitting of new Eledone hull sonar and Signaaal fire control, and the addition of a British towed array. The boats are built for quiet running with all noise-producing machinery on a rafted deck. They are therefore good passive ASW platforms. They are armed with twenty weapons, a mix of Mk 48 and NT 37C/E wire-guided homing torpedoes and Sub-Harpoon anti-ship missiles. Maximum normal diving depth is 200 metres. As modernised the 'Zwaardvis' class submarines are fully capable, modern SSKs.

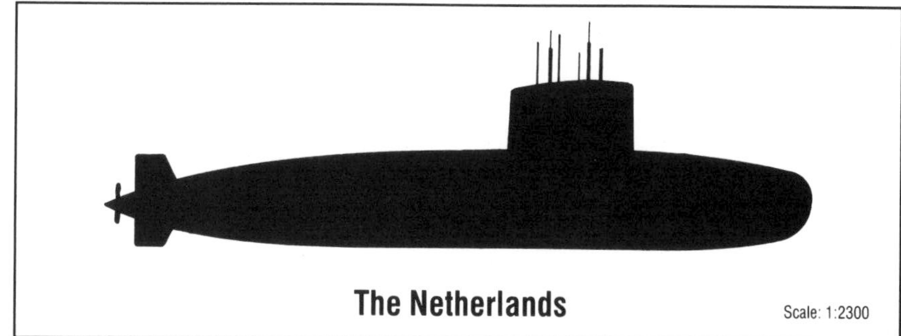

The Netherlands

Scale: 1:2300

Photograph: *Zwaardvis* (Dutch Navy)

Specifications and Technical Data

Number in class: 3

POTVIS S804 1965
TONIJN S805 1966
ZEEHOND S809 1961

Displacement, tonnes: S809 1,509, S804-5 1,831 submerged
Dimensions, metres (feet): S809 79.5 × 7.8 × 4.8, S804-5 78.3 × 7.8 × 5 (260.9/256.9 × 25.8 × 15.7/16.4)
Torpedo tubes: 8 × 533 mm 4 forward 4 stern
Sonar: hull-mounted medium-frequency passive search and attack
Radar: 1001 I band surface search
Machinery: S809 2 × MAN 12-V6V 22/30 diesels, 2,800 hp, 2 × electric motors, 4,200 hp, 2 × shafts; S804-5 2 × SEMT-Pielstick PA4 diesels, 3,100 hp, 2 × 920kW electric motors, 4,400 hp, 2 × shafts
Speed, knots: 14,5 surfaced, 17 submerged
Complement: 67

The original four members of the class were projected as early as 1949 to provide the Netherlands with its own indigenous fast battery-drive submarines. After an extended design period *Zeehond* and her sister *Dolfijn* were finally begun at Rotterdamse Droogdok at the end of 1954. They were not launched, however, until February 1960 and May 1959 respectively. The next pair were delayed by abortive negotiations with the Americans to adopt nuclear propulsion. Given lack of progress, it was decided to build two more 'Dolfijns', but with several modifications to optimise them for the ASW hunter-killer role. Both were built at Wilton-Fijenoord, Shiedam in 1962. They were launched in 1965, *Potvis* on 12 January and *Tonijn* on 14 June. The two older boats were brought up to the standards of the later pair. *Dolfijn* was stricken in 1983 and scrapped in 1985. *Zeehond* was due to follow her, but was given a major refit in the late 1980s to allow her to continue in service to replace the delayed *Walrus*. The other two will run on until they are replaced by the two later boats of the 'Walrus' class. The hull design is an interesting one with three parallel pressure cylinders, the upper containing the armament, crew and navigational equipment, and each of the lower tubes a MAN diesel and electric motor, battery cells and storage spaces. The layout gives greater stability, better space distribution, safer fuel storage and greater diving depth. The excessive length compared to the 'teardrop' layout leads, however, to greater underwater resistance.

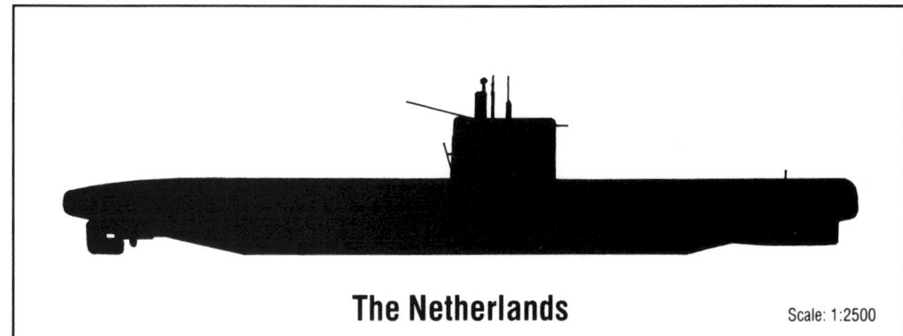

Photograph: *Tonijn* 1988 (Gary Davies/USNI)

Specifications and Technical Data

Number in class: 6

ULA S300 1989
UTSIRA S301 1992
UTSTEIN S302 1991
UTVAER S303 1990
UTHAUG S304 1991
UREDD S305 1990

Displacement, tonnes: 1,150 submerged
Dimensions, metres (feet): 59 × 5.4 × 4.6 (193.6 × 17.7 × 15.1)
Torpedo tubes: 8 × 533 mm forward
Sonar: CSU83 active/passive medium-frequency intercept, search and attack, Thomson Sinta passive low-frequency flank array
Radar: Calypso III I band surface search
Action Information Organisation: MSI-90U
Machinery: 2 × MTU 16V 652 TB 91 diesels, 5,500 hp, 1 × electric motor 6,000 hp, 1 × shaft
Speed, knots: 11 surfaced, 23 submerged
Range, nautical miles: 5,000 at 8 knots snorting
Complement: 18-20

These boats are a combined West German/Norwegian Project 2071, Type 210 in the German submarine series. Parts, including all but *Ula* hull sections, are being made in Norway for assembly at Thyssen, Nordseewerke in Germany. *Ula* was laid down on 29 January 1987 and *Ured* on 16 June 1988, *Utstein* on 8 December 1988 and *Utvaer* on 15 June 1989. *Ula* was commissioned on 27 June 1989. These boats are to replace six of the smaller 'Kobben' class and some will take the previous names and pennant numbers of the older boats. The Norwegians are providing their own command weapon control systems, but the boats will carry fourteen German AEG DM 2A3 Seeal dual-purpose wire-guided homing torpedoes. The sonar fit is Franco-German a Krupp-Atlas sonar set and Thomson-CSF passive conformal arrays. These boats are intended primarily for coastal operations, but at double the size of their predecessors they bring Norway into the SSK category. Maximum diving depth of the 'Ulas' is 250 metres and endurance 40 days. Two more were projected, but these plans have now been dropped.

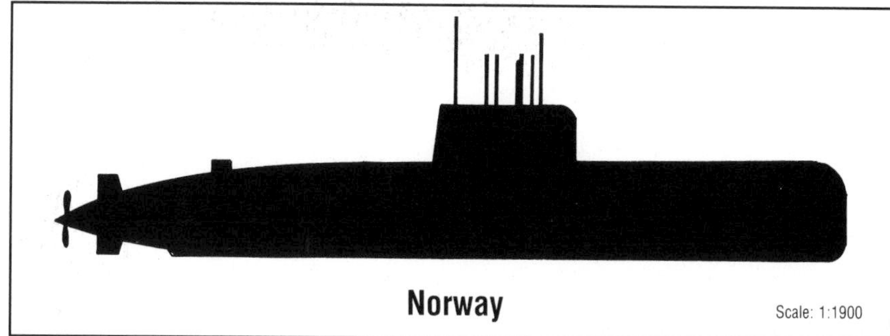

Norway

Scale: 1:1900

Photograph: *Ula* 1989 (Monch)

S306

Number in class: 13

Norway
UTSIRA S301 1965
SKOLPEN S306 1966
STADT S307 1965
STORD S308 1967
SVENNER S309 1967
SKLINNA S314 1966
KAURA S315 1965
KINN S316 1965
KOBBEN S318 1964
KUNNA S319 1964

Denmark
TUMLEREN S322 1986 (1965)
SAELEN S323 1986 (1966)
SPRINGEREN S324 1989 (1964)

Displacement, tonnes: 435 submerged
Dimensions, metres (feet): 45.4, modernised boats 47.4 × 4.6 × 4.3 (148.9/155.5 × 15 × 4)
Torpedo tubes: 8 × 533 mm forward
Sonar: Atlas medium/high-frequency passive search and attack, modified in modernised boats
Radar: Calypso II I band surface search
Action Information Organisation: MSI-70U, modernised boats M-90U
Machinery: 2 × MTU 12V 493 AZ 1,200 hp, 1 × 1,100 kW electric motor, 1,700 hp, 1 × shaft
Speed, knots: 12 surfaced, 18 submerged
Range, nautical miles: 5,000 at 8 knots snorting
Complement: 18

In 1959 the United States and Norway agreed to share equally the cost of fourteen modified versions of the new West German Type 205 coastal submarines. Designated Type 207 they were laid down at the Rheinstahl-Nordseewerke, Emden between 1963 and 1966. They have proved to be extremely effective boats in service, being almost undetectable in Norway's coastal waters. Their torpedo tubes are filled with a mix of Type 61 wire-guided anti-surface passive homing torpedos or NT37C dual-purpose wire-guided active/passive homers. Six boats are to be modernised for retention in the 1990s. This includes new sonar and fire control equipment and modified electronics. The modernisation schedule is **S314** January 1989, **S306** October 1989, **S308** August 1990, **S318** May 1991, **S319** December 1991, **S315** April 1992. Two boats (**S322-3**) have already been modified for sale to Denmark. A third boat, **S324**, the former Norwegian *Kya* is also being transferred to the Danes. The original *Stadt* (**S307**) was to have been the third Danish boat but she had to be scrapped after a grounding incident in 1987. The original *Utstein* (**S302**) was renamed and renumbered to release its original name and number for a new 'Ula' class boat. She will not be modernised and neither will the present **S301**, **S309** or **S316**. These will probably be scrapped when the new 'Ula' class boats enter service. **S316** was originally called *Ula*. The Danish boats fire Type 61 wire-guided torpedoes.

Photograph: *Skolpen* 1982 (USNI)

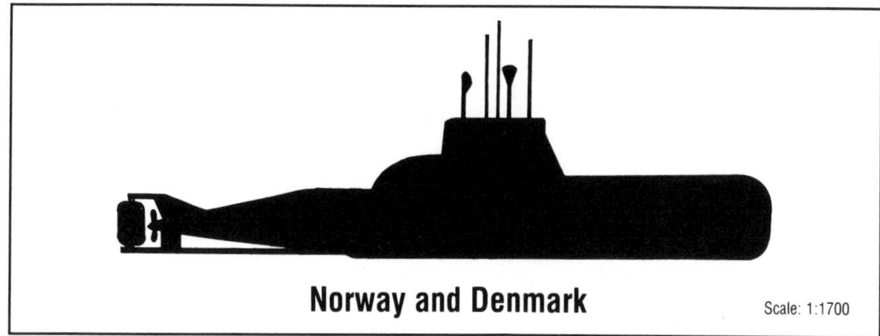

S342

Number in class: 2

HIZIR REIS S342 1980 (1952)
PIRI REIS S343 1980 (1951)

Specifications and Technical Data

Displacement, tonnes: 2,600 submerged
Dimensions, metres (feet): 87.4 × 8.3 × 5.8 (287 × 27.3 × 19)
Torpedo tubes: 8 × 533 mm, 6 forward, 2 stern
Sonar: BQR 2B passive hull-mounted medium-frequency search and attack, BQS 4 active, BQG 4 PUFFS passive ranging
Radar: BPS 12 I band surface search
Machinery: 3 × Fairbanks-Morse 38D8-1/8 diesels, 4,500 hp, 2 × electric motors, 5,600 hp, 2 × shafts
Speed, knots: 16 surfaced, 16 submerged
Range, nautical miles: 7,600 at 15 knots surfaced, 17 at 9 knots submerged
Complement: 86

The six boats of the 'Tang' class were America's first post-war fast battery-drive submarines. **S343** was laid down in the Portsmouth Navy Yard as the USS *Tang*, name boat of the class, on 18 April 1949. She was launched two years later and commissioned in October 1951. Her sister was the last of the class to be completed, being laid down as the USS *Gudgeon* at the same yard on 20 May 1950, launched on 11 June 1952 and commissioned on 21 November 1952. **S343** was leased to Turkey for five years in 1980 and commissioned into the Turkish Navy on 21 March 1980. **S342** was leased at the end of September 1983. These boats were purchased outright by the Turkish Navy in 1988. *Hizir Reis* was built with is present engine installation; *Piri Reis*, like the other first four members of the class, originally had more compact, but troublesome, radial diesels. Like the 'Guppy' conversions, these new build submarines had greatly-increased battery power for higher submerged speed. The shorter length of the 'Tangs', however, reduced underwater resistance and their underwater speed was equal to that possible on the surface. The last pair of boats were given the PUFFS passive ranging sonar to improve their anti-submarine capabilities. *Piri Reis* still carries this system. Both boats spent their last active years in the US Navy as acoustic research submarines, *Gudgeon* replacing *Tang* in this duty in April 1979. They will be replaced by the new advanced boats of German design under construction in Turkey. The stern tubes can only fire short Mk 37 torpedoes.

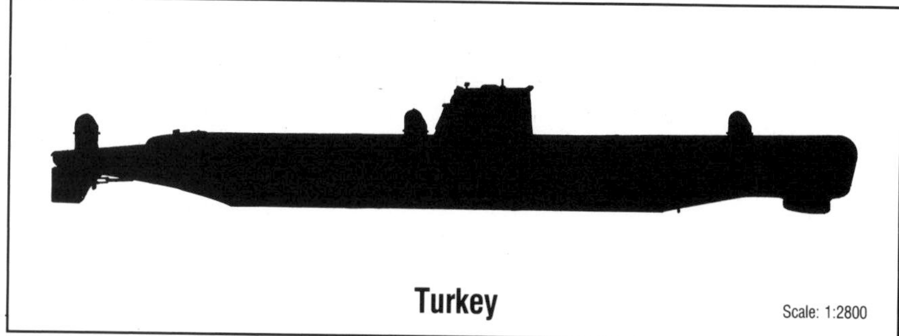
Turkey

Scale: 1:2800

Photograph: *Hizir Reis* 1987 (G Valentini/USNI)

Specifications and Technical Data

Number in class: 4

UPHOLDER S40 1990
UNSEEN S41 1990
URSULA S42 1991
UNICORN S43 1993

Displacement, tonnes: 2,455 submerged
Dimensions, metres (feet): 70.3 × 7.6 × 5.5 (230.6 × 25 × 17.7)
Torpedo tubes: 6 × 533 mm forward
Sonar: 2026 towed array, 2040 hull-mounted medium-frequency active passive search, 2007 passive low-frequency flank array, 2019 passive ranging and intercept
Radar: 1007 I band navigation
Action Information Organisation: DCC
Machinery: 2 × Paxman Valenta 1600 RPA-200 SZ diesels, 1 × GEC electric motor, 5,400 hp, 1 × shaft
Speed, knots: 12 surfaced, 20 submerged
Range, nautical miles: 8,000 at 8 knots snorting
Complement: 44

Photograph: *Upholder* (VSEL)

As early as 1974-5 a Ministry of Defence Working Party came out favour of considering a programme of new conventionally-powered submarines. Various options were considered and eventually a boat of about 2,250 tons was decided upon. Vickers, however, had produced their own design for a 2,500-ton boat for export and this was combined with the Naval Staff concept to produce the Type 2400 around which an official Naval Staff requirement was written in 1980. Board approval for the new boats was given in August 1981 but the order was not finally placed with Vickers at Barrow for the prototype until November 1983. Named *Upholder* she was launched in December 1986. The export orders did not appear, but the Royal Navy ordered three sisters from Cammell Laird at the beginning of 1986.

Upholder's acceptance into service was delayed from October 1989 to January 1990 because of problems on her trials with both her torpedo tubes and the main machinery control system. She will eventually enter service with an advanced sonar fit (the second batch is to be fitted with 2075 hull sonar) and twelve of the latest torpedoes, Tigerfish or Spearfish. The boats can also be used for minelaying, training and special forces insertion. Diving depth is 200 metres and endurance 49 days. They can stay submerged for 90 hours at 3 knots.

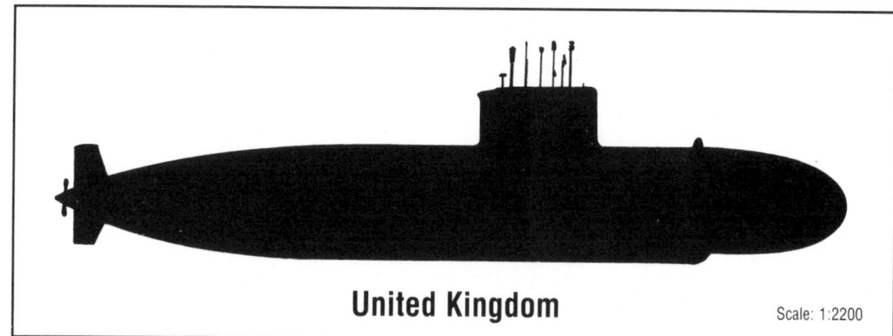

Number in class: 10

ODIN S10 1962
OSIRIS S13 1964
ONSLAUGHT S14 1962
OTTER S15 1962
ORACLE S16 1963
OCELOT S17 1964
OTUS S18 1963
OPOSSUM S19 1964
OPPORTUNE S20 1965
ONYX S21 1967

›pecifications ınd Technical Data

ʼisplacement, tonnes: 2,410 submerged
imensions, metres (feet): 90 × 8.1 × 5.5 ʔ95.2 × 26.5 × 18)
ɔrpedo tubes: 6 × 533 mm forward
ɔnar: 2024 towed array, 2051 hull-mounted ıedium-frequency active/passive search and attack, ɔ07 hull-mounted pasive flank array
adar: 1006 I band navigation
ction Information Organisation: DCH
ıachinery: 2 × Admiralty 16VMS diesels, 3,280 hp, × electric motors, 6,000 hp, 2 × shafts
peed, knots: 12 surfaced, 17 submerged
ange, nautical miles: 9,000 at 12 knots
ɔmplement: 69

fter World War II Britain designed a new fast battery-ʼive submarine based on German concepts, but ɔnsiderably modified to suit national practice. The ısult was the 'Porpoise' class, eight of which were laid ɔwn between 1955 and 1958. All are now ɛcommissioned but the design, already noted as one of e quietest of its day, was further developed into the ʼberon' class, the first of which was laid down at ıatham dockyard in 1957. The new boats, as well as ɛing even quieter, had increased diving depth, down to ıout 300 metres when new. They are still effective SKs. Three unmodernised 'Oberons' have been taken ıt of service, but the ten remaining boats are being ɔdernised with new sonar, fire control systems and ɛctronic warfare equipment. The original bow sonar as the 187 medium-frequency active/passive set: 2 torpedo tubes for short anti-escort weapons were also fitted aft, but these are now removed. This will maintain their operational capability into the 1990s when they will be slowly phased out of service and probably sold abroad. The class has already proved popular in the export market with six going to Australia, three to Canada, three to Brazil and two to Chile. Builders and launch dates were *Odin*, Cammell Laird, Birkenhead, 1960; *Osiris*, Vickers, Barrow, 1962; *Onslaught*, Chatham Dockyard, 1950; *Otter*, Scotts, Greenock, 1961; *Oracle*, Cammell Laird, Birkenhead, 1961; *Ocelot*, Chatham Dockyard, 1962; *Otus*, Scotts, Greenock 1962; *Opossum*, Cammell Laird, Birkenhead, 1963; *Opportune*, Scotts, Greenock, 1963; *Onyx*, Cammell Laird, Birkenhead, 1966. The original *Onyx* was purchased by the Canadians and a new boat added to the programme.

Photograph: *Opossum* 1984 (M Lennon/USNI)

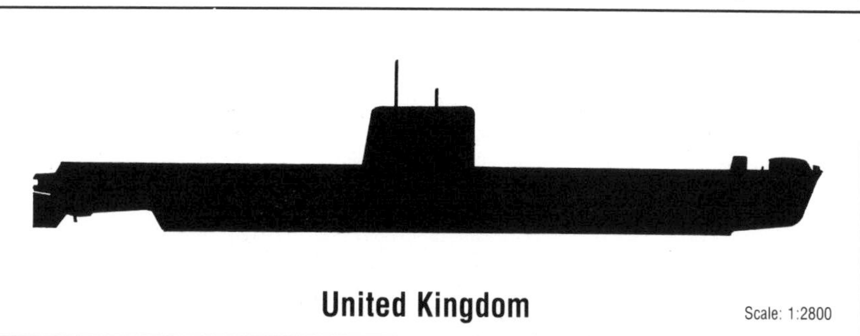
United Kingdom
Scale: 1:2800

Number in class: 1

FOUDRE L9011 1991

Landing Ship Dock Foudre TCD (TCD90) Class

Specifications and Technical Data

Displacement, tonnes: 11,800 full load
Dimensions, metres (feet): 168 × 23.5 × 52/9.2 flooded (551 × 77.1 × 17/30.2)
Guns: 1 × 2 40 mm forward, 2 × 2 20 mm aft
Aircraft: 4 × Super Puma
Missiles: 2 × 6 SADRAL launchers for Mistral missiles
Military lift: 470 troops plus 1810 tons equipment
Radar: RM1229 I band navigation
Machinery: 2 × SEMT-Pielstick 16 PC 2.5 V400 diesels, 21,600 hp, 2 × shafts
Speed, knots: 21
Range, nautical miles: 11,000 at 15 knots
Complement: 210

The first of a new class of TCD (Transport de Chalands de Débarquement) was ordered at the end of 1984. Two more were announced in 1986 and 1988, but these have since been deferred and will not be built until France's existing pair of TCDs come to the end of their lives in the 1990s. The ships can carry either ten LCM small landing craft or two larger LCTs. Alternatively, a 450 ton P400 patrol vessel may be carried in the dock. Helicopter facilities are extensive with a hangar for four large helicopters and three landing spots. The ship was designed to take a regiment of the Force d'Action Rapide, but she can also be used as a transport carrying up to 1,200 troops. She also contains command facilities and a hospital. *Foudre* was laid down at the Naval Dockyard, Brest on 26 March 1986 and was launched on 19 November 1988. In 1988 France commissioned a smaller dock landing ship, *Bougainville*, especially for use in support of her nuclear tests in the Pacific. She carries a landing ship pennant number, L9011.

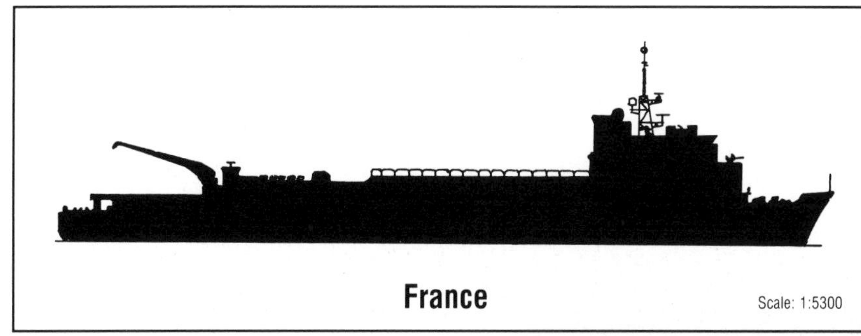

Photograph: *Foudre* official model (DCN/USNI)

L9021

Ouragan Class

Number in class: 2

OURAGAN L9021 1965
ORAGE L9022 1968

Specifications and Technical Data

Displacement, tonnes: 8,500 full load
Dimensions, metres (feet): 149 × 23 × 5.4/8.7 flooded (488.9 × 75.4 × 17.7/28.5)
Aircraft: flight deck for 10 × Alouette, 3 or 4 × Super Frélon helicopters
Guns: 2 × 1 120 mm mortars, 4 × 1 40mm
Military lift: 472 troops plus 1,500 tons stores
Sonar: SQS17 medium-frequency search (L9021 only)
Radar: Decca 1226 I band navigation
Machinery: 2 × SEMT-Pielstick diesels, 8,600 hp, 2 × shafts
Speed, knots: 17
Range, nautical miles: 9,000
Complement: 238

These ships, designated Transports de Chalands de Débarquement (TCDs) were designed both to lift a battalion of naval infantry and its support troops by helicopter and to put ashore troops and heavy support by landing craft. For the latter role they can carry two 635-ton LCTs each with a capacity of eleven light tanks or eighteen smaller LCM(6)s. The dock is 120 metres long and floods to 3 metres. They do not have a hangar, but can either operate helicopters from their large flight deck or carry helicopters in the open. Up to four large or thirteen small helicopters can be operated. The flight deck can be varied in size using removable sections and the internal stowage deck can also be extended, reducing the docking space. As a logisitics transport the ships can carry 18 large helicopters or 80 small helicopters, 120 light tanks, 84 DWKWs, 340 jeeps, or 12 50-ton barges. 349 troops can be carried, 470 for short distances. The superstructure is mounted on the starboard side rather like that of an aircraft carrier. They can also double as repair ships. *Orage* was assigned to the nuclear test centre in the Pacific until relieved by *Bougainville*. She is returning to service in her designed role. Both ships are assigned to the Atlantic Fleet. They will be life-expired in 1990 and 1993, but they will probably serve on until replaced by the projected members of the 'Foudre' class. The 'Ouragans' were both built in the Naval Dockyard, Brest being laid down in June 1962 and June 1966. They were launched in November 1963 and April 1967.

Photograph: *Ouragan* 1983 (van Ginderen/USNI)

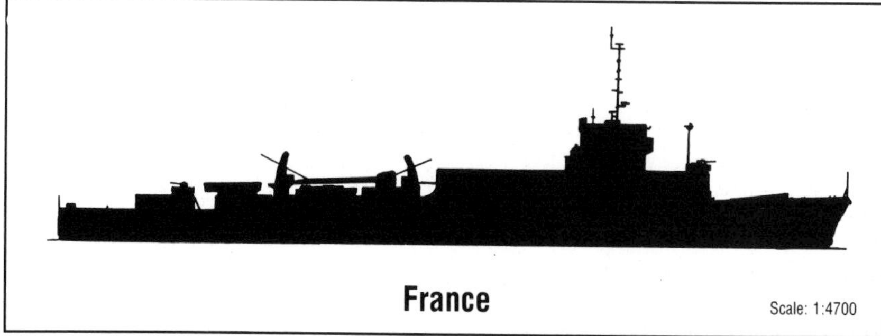

France

Scale: 1:4700

L153

Number in class: 1

NAFKRATOUSSA L1553 1971 (1945)

Specifications and Technical Data

Displacement, tonnes: 9,375 full load
Dimensions, metres (feet): 139.6 × 20.2 × 5.5 (457.8 × 72.2 × 18)
Aircraft: platform for light helicopter
Guns: 2 × 4 40 mm on each side of bridge, 4 × 2 20 mm on each beam forward
Radar: SPS 6 D band air search, SPS 5 G/H band surface search
Machinery: 2 × sets geared steam turbines, 7,000 hp, 2 × shafts
Military Lift: 137 troops, 1,347 tons stores
Speed, knots: 15
Range, nautical miles: 8,000 at 12 knots
Complement: 250

During World War II the Americans, working to a British staff requirement, originated the Landing Ship Dock or LSD. The concept was a self-propelled dry dock capable of moving combat-loaded small landing craft over oceanic distances. Some 27 were built of which four were lent to the Royal Navy. The first eight, the 'Ashland' class, had reciprocating steam engines, the rest, known as the 'Cabildo' class, had steam turbines. *Navkratoussa* was built as the USS *Fort Mandan* LSD21, laid down at Boston Navy Yard in December 1944 and launched on 6 April 1945. She was completed on 31 October 1945 just too late to see service in the war. Post-war the LSDs were fitted with helicopter platforms, and in the early 1960s, *Fort Mandan* was one of the five 'Cabildo' class LSDs to be given a fleet rehabilitation and modernisation programme (FRAM II) conversion. She was leased to the Greeks in 1971 and sold to them in February 1980. She serves as the flagship of the Greek Captain Landing Forces. She can carry up to eighteen small 56 ton LCMs in her dock and each with a smaller LCVP embarked in it Spain operated a vessel of this class from 1971 to 1988, the *Galicia* formerly USS *San Marcos* (LSD 25).

Photograph: *Nafkratoussa* (Greek Navy)

L 9893

San Giorgio Class

Number in class: 2

SAN GIORGIO L9892 1987
SAN MARCO L9893 1988

Specifications and Technical Data

Displacement, tonnes: 7,665 full load
Dimensions, metres (feet): 133.3 × 20.5 × 5.3 (437.2 × 67.3 × 17.4)
Aircraft: up to 5 × Chinook or Sea King helicopters stowed on flight deck
Guns: 1 × 1 76 mm forward, 2 × 1 20mm, 2 × 1 12.7 mm
Military lift: Battalion plus up to 30 tanks and 36 armoured personnel carriers plus 399 cubic metres of stores
Radar: SPS 702 I band surface search
Machinery: 2 × GMT A420.12 diesels, 16,800 hp, 2 × shafts
Speed, knots: 20
Range, nautical miles: 7,500 at 16 knots, 4,500 at 20 knots
Complement: 170

San Giorgio was ordered in November 1983 and laid down at the Fincantieri yard at Riva Trigoso on 27 June 1985. She was launched on 25 February 1987. *San Marco* was ordered on 5 March 1984 and was paid for by the Ministry of Civil Protection as a disaster relief ship. She was laid down at Riva Trigoso on 28 June 1986 and launched on 21 October 1987. She has more extensive hospital facilities than her sister ship. Both vessels were fitted out at Fincantieri, Muggiano. *San Marco* will revert to naval command in any military crisis and both ships form part of the Third Naval Division at Brindisi. The armoured personnel carriers are stored in a vehicle hangar below the flight deck which is connected to the hangar by a 30-ton elevator. The flight deck can be used for storing three 11-ton LCVPs. Three 65-ton LCMs specially built for the ships are carried in the aft docking well. Unlike most LPDs these ships can be beached and have a bow ramp. The acquisition of these versatile vessels gives the Italian Navy a considerable improvement in its amphibious capability and a useful intervention capacity both in and out of the NATO area.

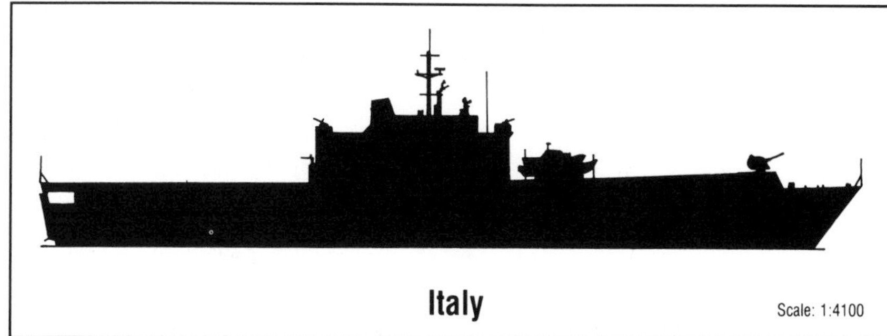

Photograph: *San Marco* 1988 (L Grazioli/USNI)

L11

Number in class: 2

FEARLESS L10 1965
INTREPID L11 1967

Specifications and Technical Data

Displacement, tonnes: 12,120 full load
Dimensions, metres (feet): 158.5 × 24.4 × 6.2/9.8 flooded (520 × 80 × 20.5/32)
Aircraft: platform for 5 × Sea King helicopters
Missiles: SAM: Seacat GWS20 quadruple launchers on each beam forward
Guns: 2 × 1 40 mm in bridge wings, 2 × 2 30 mm on after superstructure (being replaced by 20 mm Vulcan Phalanx CIWS in *Fearless*), 2 × 1 20 mm forward
Military lift: up to 400 troops and 12 tanks
Radar: 994 E/F band surface searh, 1006 I band navigation
Machinery: 2 × sets English Electric geared steam turbines, 22,000 hp, 2 × shafts
Speed, knots: 21
Range, nautical miles: 5,000 at 20 knots
Complement: 660

A Landing Ship Dock was projected by the Royal Navy in the immediate post-war period, but funds were never available and it was not until 1962 at the height of Britain's East of Suez strategy that two vessels were laid down on the lines of contemporary American LPDs (Landing Platform Dock), *Fearless* was built by Harland and Wolff, Belfast and was launched on 19 December 1963. *Intrepid* was constructed at John Brown, Clydebank and was launched on 25 June 1964. The ships have led active lives around the world although their main role since 1971 has been on the flanks of NATO. They were to have been paid off after the 1981 Defence Review but it was decided to retain them in service and they played a leading part in the Falklands War. They are, however, very manpower-intensive ships and one is normally kept in reserve. The vessels carry four 170-ton LCU Mk 9 landing craft in their dock and smaller LCVPs on davits. The ships have comprehensive command facilities with an assault operations room that can act as Brigade Headquarters. On refit *Fearless* is acquiring a NAUTIS-L action data/navigation. The need for these command facilities has been an important factor in obtaining government authorisation for the replacement or service life extension of these ships. A firm decision on this may finally be taken in 1990. In addition tenders are being studied for a 25,000 ton Aviation Support Ship that will supplement the LPDs and provide sufficient helicopter spots for a three company lift. This decision is also expected in 1990.

Photograph: *Intrepid* 1989 (W Sartori)

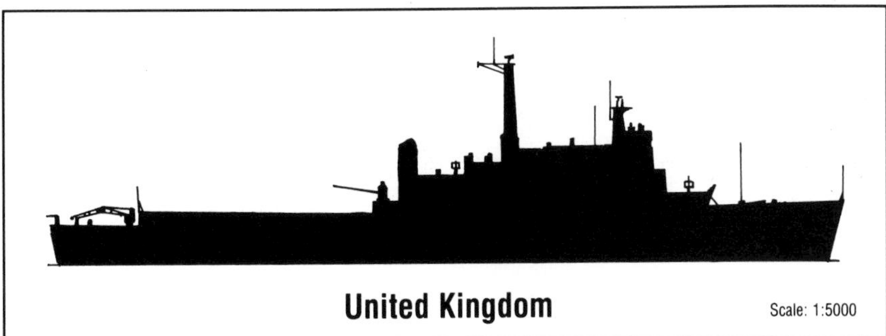

Index of Vessels and Classes

Index of Pennant Numbers